Marina Druker

Enchanting Toys
& Soft Sculptures

Sculpting • Crazy Quilting • Embellishing • Embroidery

C&T PUBLISHING

Text and How-To Photography copyright © 2012 by Marina Druker

Photography and Artwork copyright © 2012 by C&T Publishing, Inc.

Publisher: Amy Marson

Creative Director: Gailen Runge

Art Director: Kristy Zacharias

Editor: Cynthia Bix

Technical Editors: Ann Haley and Priscilla Read

Cover/Book Designer: April Mostek

Production Coordinator: Zinnia Heinzmann

Production Editor: Alice Mace Nakanishi

Illustrator: Kirstie L. Pettersen

Photography by Christina Carty-Francis and Diane Pedersen of C&T Publishing, Inc., unless otherwise noted

Published by C&T Publishing, Inc., P.O. Box 1456, Lafayette, CA 94549

Library of Congress Cataloging-in-Publication Data

Druker, Marina, 1975-

Enchanting art dolls & soft sculptures : sculpting-crazy quilting-embellishing-embroidery / Marina Druker.

pages cm

ISBN 978-1-60705-529-7 (soft cover)

1. Dollmaking. 2. Soft sculpture. I. Title.

TT175.D78 2012

745.592--dc23

2011046638

Printed in China

10 9 8 7 6 5 4 3 2 1

Acknowledgments

Special thanks to my husband and my son for their love and their acceptance of the difficulties involved in living with a creative person. Thanks also to my family and friends for their support and encouragement.

Many thanks to the artists who took time to share photos of their amazing dolls and other works in this book and to the photographers for the use of their photographs.

Special thanks to Alika Kalaida for her valuable advice on writing and editing my book and for her kind words; and to Doris Brant, who is a great friend and whose faith kept the project moving forward.

Also thank you to Susanne Woods, acquisitions editor at C&T Publishing, for asking me to write this book; to Cynthia Bix, developmental editor, who worked with me on the manuscript; and to the whole team at C&T Publishing, who helped make this book the best it could be.

contents

Discovering the Art of Dolls   4

Essential Tools and Materials   8

Doll-Making Basics   11

Crazy Quilting Doll Costumes and Soft Sculptures   21

PROJECTS

Cinderella Princess Doll   27

Rose Fairy Doll   35

Mermaid on a Patchwork Sea   41

Butterfly Doll in a Frame   45

Brooch Doll Trio   49

Fantasy Fish   52

Elegant Teddy Bear   55

Enchanted Cottage   59

Doll Gallery   62

Template Patterns   78

Resources   87

About the Author   87

Discovering the Art of Dolls

From the time I was a child growing up in St. Petersburg, Russia, I tried my hand at nearly every kind of decorative art, including sculpting, drawing, embroidery, and sewing. Fabrics were always of special interest to me. My grandmother sewed clothes, so I was always surrounded by beautiful fabric, buttons, and other sewing notions. When I discovered doll making and began to create dolls that featured crazy quilting, I knew that I had found a unique way to combine all kinds of decorative art—working with three-dimensional models and with color, as well as drawing and needlework.

A Brief History

Every doll is a unique object; people have felt the impulse to create these small figures throughout human history. Archaeologists have found doll-like figures made more than 4,000 years ago.

In fifteenth-century Germany, craftsmen made some of the earliest dolls for children. These were carved from wood, painted, and costumed. Porcelain dolls with cloth and leather bodies appeared in the eighteenth century. Doll costumes became very elaborate, and costumed dolls sometimes acted as the fashion magazines of the time. French dressmakers sewed small replicas of fashionable clothes and sent them to different countries in order to popularize French fashions abroad.

Throughout history, people have also made cloth dolls or rag dolls and toys, stuffed with straw, beans, cotton, or in modern times, synthetic stuffing. Usually these were handmade for children to play with. The first successful commercial stuffed toys were made in the 1880s in Germany by the Steiff Company, which later originated the teddy bear.

As the doll industry continued to develop, new doll-making materials appeared. Papier-mâché was invented in the early nineteenth century, and this material made it possible to mass-produce dolls. By the middle of the twentieth century, rubber and plastic became the most popular materials for making mass-produced dolls.

Although dolls have long been made as toys for children, handmade art dolls have emerged as a relatively new genre of contemporary fine art. Today's air-hardening modeling materials, such as Creative Paperclay and others, now make it easy for any crafter or artist to mold unique dolls without the need for firing in a kiln or oven. Doll makers can create one-of-a-kind dolls from start to finish, using and combining a variety of mediums. All over the world, there are many associations and organizations for professional and nonprofessional doll makers. Every year hundreds of exhibitions attract large numbers of visitors—both artists and collectors.

Making Dolls

My soft fabric creations are made from crazy-quilted and embellished fabrics, while my sculpted dolls have molded faces, hands, and feet and a padded wire body framework on which I "build" the crazy-quilted costumes. I made my first doll with a crazy-quilted costume while I was planning a birthday gift for myself—a doll I called *Pisces,* in honor of my birth sign. I had long been attracted to the unique look of crazy quilting, and I had been collecting pictures of crazy-quilted pieces, beautiful stitches, and interesting motifs. As I planned this doll, all of these elements suddenly came together. This small doll paved the way for my Zodiac Collection of dolls, as well as the Seasons Collection doll series. For the Zodiac Collection, I created a different doll to represent each astrological sign; the whole project took me about a year to complete. To see these doll collections, visit my website, www.miopupazzo.com.

Pisces, from the Zodiac Collection, designed and made by Marina Druker

Over the years, as I've made many dolls, I have found my own style. My sculpted dolls have rather plain, simple faces, without intricately molded facial features or heavy paint—just simply formed eyes, noses, and mouths, enhanced with light color to suggest personality. Their costumes are crazy quilted and embellished with embroidery, fanciful charms, and other pretty things.

I have been collecting materials for a long time, and my supply of fabrics, lace, buttons, and beads is constantly being replenished. Friends and sometimes even strangers contribute indispensable help by donating scraps of fabric, lace, and other embellishments. Many of these scraps are very special to me. More than 30 years ago, my grandmother made a dress of emerald floral fabric. A black-and-white snapshot is the only reminder of the dress; however, scraps of the fabric live on in the dress of a doll called *Summer* that I created for my Seasons Collection.

Summer, *from the Seasons Collection, designed and made by Marina Druker*

Butterfly Doll in a Frame *(project on page 45)*

In addition to making freestanding dolls, I love to create dolls mounted on decorated frames, such as *Butterfly Doll in a Frame* (page 45). The frame and background complement the doll and turn it into three-dimensional wall art. A framed doll makes a lovely gift; you can personalize it by decorating the frame and creating a background with elements that fit the recipient's tastes— lines of poetry, music, old photographs, favorite recipes. As an added benefit, framed dolls can be displayed on a wall instead of taking up space on a shelf or tabletop.

Fantasy Fish *(project on page 52)*

I also enjoy making sewn and stuffed creations that have crazy-quilted surfaces, such as *Fantasy Fish* (page 52). Like the dolls, these are not children's toys but art pieces handmade from special fabrics and lavishly embellished.

If you would like to try your hand at creating either kind of doll or soft sculpture, you will find that doll making is a very exciting process. First there is the concept; your doll can be a portrait of a real person or a fantasy figure. Choose an image that truly appeals to you and that you think you can successfully represent. To execute your vision, you will need to combine many skills. If you decide to make a sculpted doll, you'll mold and paint it, make hair, create a body, sew apparel, and add suitable accessories. For a soft sculpture, you will need various sewing and needlework skills. Although you can't expect to master all of these skills right away, especially if many are new to you, you will find that with every piece you make comes experience, added proficiency, and a sense of personal achievement.

About This Book

This book will help you with every aspect of doll making, from sculpting to painting to making crazy-quilted creations. In Essential Tools and Materials (page 8) and Doll-Making Basics (page 11), you will find a description of what you need to get started, as well as step-by-step instructions for working with modeling materials and painting. Crazy Quilting Doll Costumes and Soft Sculptures (page 21) includes a discussion of fabrics and embellishments, along with steps for crazy quilting. Instructions for making various kinds of wire body frameworks, as well as for piecing and sewing soft sculptures, can be found in the individual projects. At the back of the book, you'll find full-size template patterns for the projects.

It's important to note that every sculpted doll is unique; therefore in the projects you will not find exact dimensions for the dolls. Patterns for the doll clothing are approximately sized; you will need to make your own adjustments to the templates provided, based on your particular doll. For the soft stuffed projects such as *Elegant Teddy Bear* (page 55), dimensions are more exact.

As you plan your projects, your own ideas will add something very personal to your creations. You and only you can create your own vision. If your first experience isn't as successful as expected, don't worry—just keep on trying. Remember that even the greatest artists had to start somewhere!

Essential Tools and Materials

The projects in this book include dolls such as *Cinderella Princess Doll* (page 27) and *Butterfly Doll in a Frame* (page 45), which are sculpted from air-hardening modeling material and wire; and soft fabric projects such as *Elegant Teddy Bear* (page 55) and *Fantasy Fish* (page 52), which are sewn and stuffed. All projects feature surfaces or costumes made using crazy-quilting techniques. In this chapter, you will find information about the basic tools and materials you'll need to make these projects, along with techniques for making the sculpted dolls. For information about fabrics, interfacings, and embellishments, see Crazy Quilting Doll Costumes and Soft Sculptures (page 21).

Note: *Most of the materials and tools listed may be available in your local craft and art supply stores. For a list of suppliers, see Resources (page 87).*

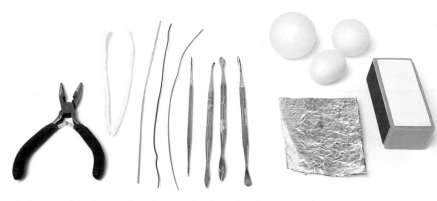

Sculpting and finishing tools and materials: Pliers, chenille stems, craft wire, modeling tools, foam balls, foil, four-way nail buffing block

Modeling Materials

With the large variety of modeling materials available to doll makers today, art dolls have become very easy to produce at home. Professional-quality air-hardening materials for sculpting include Creative Paperclay; LaDoll, LaDoll Premix, and LaDoll Premier; Darwi Classic; and FIMOair. Air-hardening materials may contain clay or may be a mixture of extender and paper pulp with the properties of fine clay. They are easy to use, nontoxic, fast drying, and lightweight, and they do not require firing or baking. When dry, these materials can be painted, carved, stamped, and sanded. One shortcoming of these products is their fragility; features like fingers, feet, and legs require a wire skeleton inside to make them sturdy. The materials also shrink as they dry, so cracks may occur.

Additional Materials and Tools

Listed here are tools and materials you will need to make the projects in this book. These are the essentials; there are many others that are helpful to have, and as you gain experience in doll making, you can add any that you find useful.

CRAFT WIRE   You will use craft wire of various gauges to create a framework for your doll's body. The wire should be strong but highly flexible to give the desired shape. Use medium-heavy, 16- to 22-gauge wire for the body framework and thin, 20- to 24-gauge wire for fingers or to create the body framework for small dolls. The amount of wire you need depends on the size of the doll you want to create. Use needle-nose pliers with cutters to cut and twist the wire.

CHENILLE STEMS (pipe cleaners)   These are very useful for connecting and wrapping the wire parts of the doll's framework.

POLYSTYRENE FOAM BALLS (such as Styrofoam)   Ball and egg shapes of different sizes will form the base for your doll's head. (Using a base saves modeling material.) You will cover the foam ball with aluminum foil.

SCULPTING TOOLS   An array of small tools—including sculpting tools, wax carvers, pottery tools, and dental picks—can be used for sculpting the face and other fine details of the doll. Usually tools are offered in sets. Sculpting tools are made of wood or stainless steel. Combination sculpting tools have two shaped heads, such as a rounded, tapered, or pointed tip on one end and a sharp cutting edge on the other end. You can even use ordinary knitting needles and crochet hooks of various sizes for modeling and shaping.

SANDPAPER   Once your sculpted pieces are dry, use sandpaper to remove any rough texture from the surface and achieve a smooth finish. You will start with coarse sandpaper and finish with finer sandpaper. I recommend using an ordinary four-way nail buffing block, which has surfaces for coarse sanding and fine polishing. The abrasives are mounted on a flexible plastic base that allows you to sand small details. You can even wash and reuse the block.

Painting and finishing supplies: Acrylic paints, watercolor pencils, pastels, brushes, sponges, doll hair, doll eyelashes, doll stand, textile glue, needles, thread, polyester stuffing

PAINTS   Air-hardening material will accept acrylic or watercolor paints, pastels, and even colored pencil. Protect the color with an acrylic varnish spray. Companies such as Plaid and DecoArt produce complete lines of all-purpose, premium-quality acrylic paints and varnish. Faber-Castell offers fine-quality watercolor pencils and soft pastels in all colors.

VARNISH   Use a matte varnish to seal the painted surfaces of your doll. You can also use glossy varnish to highlight lips and eyes. I use DecoArt Americana spray varnish, but there are many suitable kinds.

BRUSHES and SPONGES   Paint your doll's face and limbs using brushes of various sizes and shapes. Use flat or round brushes that are wide (sizes 6–10) to apply allover color to the surface and liner brushes (sizes between 2/0 and 2) to draw details such as eyes. You can also use small sponges to apply allover skin color.

POLYESTER STUFFING and BATTING   Use small strips of very thin batting over the wire framework to shape and fill out doll bodies, or use stuffing to fill soft sculptures like *Elegant Teddy Bear* (page 55).

DOLL HAIR   You can use many different kinds of materials for a doll's hair. Doll-making suppliers offer doll hair made of natural wool, mohair, or synthetic, in straight strands or curls. Or you can choose from an array of yarns and crochet threads. I prefer to use all sorts of threads and yarns for a greater variety of textures and colors. You can mix several colors for one head of hair, or you can buy multicolored yarn. Yarn is also useful for decorating the doll costumes.

The hair for Cinderella Princess Doll *(page 27) is curly wool yarn in mixed shades of golden blond.*

DOLL EYELASHES   Doll-making suppliers offer eyelash strips, made of mohair or synthetic fiber, in various colors.

DOLL STAND   If you want to display your doll on a stand, you can purchase a wood base in one of many different sizes and shapes. Dolls with legs and feet made of modeling material on wire can be attached to the stand by drilling small holes in the wooden base and inserting the wires.

TEXTILE GLUE   Use glue such as Gutermann Creativ HT2 Textile Glue to apply lace, ribbons, and other trims to your crazy-quilted surfaces wherever it's impractical to attach by sewing.

SCISSORS, PINS, and NEEDLES   In addition to scissors and pins, you will need a small sharps needle for sewing, a thin beading needle, and a very long needle for assembling the bodies of soft sculptures.

Doll-Making Basics

Every handmade doll (including each one you make from a project in this book) is unique. Nevertheless, the basic principles for working with the materials to form the doll's components are essentially the same. In this chapter, you'll find step-by-step instructions for sculpting a doll head, hands, and feet from air-hardening modeling material, as well as general advice on painting. Instructions for creating the doll body framework are a little different for each project; these can be found in the individual projects.

Most often the doll's head, arms, and legs are sculpted separately and connected by a wire skeleton. In general, all the parts of the doll's body that will show are sculpted, while the parts that will be hidden underneath clothing are made from wire, chenille stems, and stuffing. This saves modeling material and gives you more flexibility when making the doll's clothes.

Designing the Doll

What kind of doll do you envision? Before you begin, decide whether you want to create a realistic doll or a fantasy character. Realistic portrait dolls are based on images of real people, with true-to-life proportions and facial features. Creating these dolls usually requires a professional knowledge of sculpture and a great deal of experience. Fantasy dolls, on the other hand, are the fruit of the maker's imagination, even though the dolls have human characteristics. For inspiration, look at the range of wonderful realistic and fantasy dolls pictured in the Doll Gallery (page 62).

A variety of dolls designed and made by the author

In planning your doll, consider the following options.

GENDER and AGE   Will you make a male or female, a child or an adult? For tips on how to create the appearance of different ages in dolls, see Proportion (at right).

POSE   Will the doll be in a standing position? It could be freestanding, like *Rose Fairy Doll* (page 35), or on a stand, like *Cinderella Princess Doll* (page 27). Or it might be sitting or in some other pose. Try making a sketch to get your vision just right, especially if the pose is complex.

PERSONALITY and CHARACTER   This is where you can really use your imagination. Facial features, hair, and of course costuming all contribute to the doll's character and personality. Again, you can experiment with sketching a look for your doll.

SIZE   Although the sizes of art dolls vary widely, they are usually about 7″–24″ tall. I like to create small dolls, about 8″–12′″ tall. No two dolls will be exactly the same size; when you make your own version of the projects in this book, the size will be a little different from mine. That's part of what makes it your own.

Sculpting the Doll

In this section you will find general directions for sculpting a basic head, hands, and feet. The individual projects in this book will walk you through variations and details of these processes that apply specifically to each project. If you are new to sculpting, it's a good idea to buy some inexpensive modeling clay like Plasticine and practice, practice, practice before moving on to your chosen project.

Proportion

Even the most fanciful doll needs to have fairly realistic head and body proportions in order to look balanced and recognizable as a human figure. There are plenty of resources for artists and sculptors that provide detailed descriptions of human proportions. Books like *Drawing the Human Body: An Anatomical Guide* by Giovanni Civardi can offer guidance. For other suggestions, see Resources (page 87).

In general, the head of an average woman is one-seventh of her total height; a man's is one-eighth. The length of the arms and legs is approximately three times the head height; women's arms and legs are usually proportionately shorter than those of men. The elbow is above the waist. The hand is half as wide as the face, and the length of the hand is about two-thirds the length of the head.

Children's proportions are different; for example, a three- or four-year-old child is about five heads tall. A child's head is larger in proportion to the body than an adult's.

By slightly changing proportions, you can create different characters. A heroic or mythical figure can be taller than an average person—perhaps ten heads tall. A figure with an exaggeratedly large head and small body suggests a comic or cartoonish character, whereas an elongated body and slim legs impart elegance.

Usually the proportions of my dolls are closer to those of a child's body, with heads one-quarter to one-fifth of the total height.

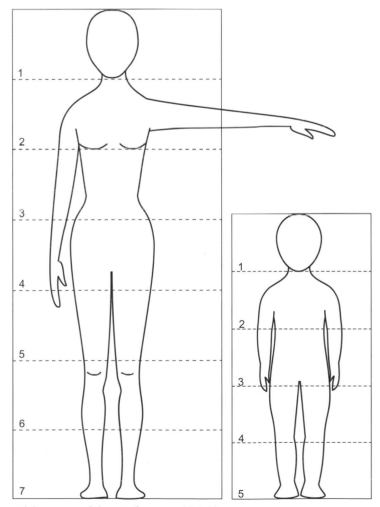

Adult woman and three- to four-year-old child

sculpting tips

In general, follow the manufacturer's directions to work with modeling materials. I also offer the following tips.

* Before sculpting, soften the modeling material in water; then knead it until it is a smooth, elastic mass. Be careful not to get it too wet; excess water can lead to cracking as it dries. However, if cracks do appear, you can easily repair them by applying a small piece of the moistened material.

* Keep the bulk of the material covered with plastic food wrap as you work, to prevent the material from drying out and losing its elasticity.

* The sculpting material is very easy to work using your fingers or sculpting tools. You can add new details to a fully dried piece by sculpting them separately and slightly moistening the place on the dried piece where you want to join them.

* Keep your hands clean; wash them from time to time as you work to remove pieces of dried modeling material.

* Let your finished work dry completely. Drying time depends on the thickness of the material, the dimensions of the details, and the ambient temperature. Times can range from a few hours for small parts up to several days for large items, such as the head. As the work dries, the color changes from slightly gray to white. When dried, the material is similar to a soft wood.

* If the head or another part is not finished in one session, you can carefully wrap it in plastic food wrap to keep it moist. Then you can return to work on it the next day.

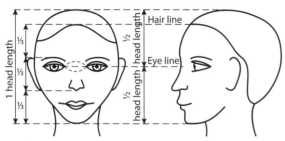

Tip *eeeeeeeeeeeeeee*

As you sculpt the head, it is very important to check it from different viewpoints—from left and right sides, from front, below, and behind—to make sure features seem balanced. Looking at the doll head reflected in a mirror sometimes helps you spot mistakes. This will allow you to make changes before the modeling material has dried.

Head proportions

Labels in diagram: Hair line, Eye line, 1 head length, ⅓, ⅓, ⅓, ⅓, ½ head length, ½ head length

Wrap basic foam ball in foil.

Photo by Eduard Druker

Head base with eye sockets

Making the Head

Observing real people is a good way to start envisioning your doll's head and face. Look at yourself in the mirror—profile as well as frontal views. Although everybody's face has the same elements—nose, mouth, two eyes, and two ears—it is amazing how much variety there can be in how people look. Age, gender, and ethnicity are just some of the elements that can affect the basic look of facial features. For example, noses can be long or short, wide or narrow, or perhaps turned up a little at the tip. Eyes may have a round, almond, or other shape; lips can be full or thin, heart-shaped or downturned. Facial expression is also important. Study images of people exhibiting various emotions—joy, surprise, sadness, laughter. All emotions affect the appearance of the eyes and mouth, and even the cheeks.

When you begin to sculpt, consider head and facial proportions, keeping in mind the following guidelines.

* In most cases, the head is egg-shaped, and the left and right sides are of equal size and symmetrical shape. The back of the head should not be flat. And of course, the face has contours; facial features like cheeks, forehead, and chin protrude.

* An imaginary horizontal line at eye level divides the face in half. Eyes are equally sized and equidistant from the vertical center line of the face. The eyeballs are spherical and set into eye sockets.

* The nose is roughly a triangle, narrow at the top and wide at the bottom.

* The mouth is halfway between the nose and the chin.

* The ears are positioned at a level midway between the line of the eyebrows and the bottom of the nose.

1. Wrap the foam ball or foam egg tightly in a layer of foil, molding it to a rough egg shape. Be aware that the completed head will be about one-third larger than the base once it is covered with modeling material.

2. Cover the head base with modeling material to about ¼″ thick, pressing it firmly onto the head base. To form the forehead, cheeks, and chin, moisten the appropriate areas and add additional small pieces of the material. Smooth and gently shape them. Above the cheeks, press gently with your finger to create depressions for the eye sockets.

3. For the nose, create a cone shape from a small piece of modeling material. Moisten the place where it will be added, and affix it firmly in place. With your fingers and the rounded end of a sculpting tool, shape the nose a little and thoroughly smooth the uneven parts so that no raw edges are visible.

Smooth and sculpt the nose.

4. Roll out a thin piece of modeling material for the lips, and place it on a moistened area under the nose.

Add the lips.

5. To create more detail on the mouth, use the sharp edge of a sculpting tool to split the lips along the middle. Other tools, such as a toothpick, can be very useful for such fine facial features as shaping the upper and lower lips and creating details on their surfaces. Use the rounded end of the sculpting tool to gently create holes for nostrils. This will flare them out a little for a more realistic look. Pressing a vertical indentation from the nose to the center top lip gives the area added definition.

Make holes for nostrils.

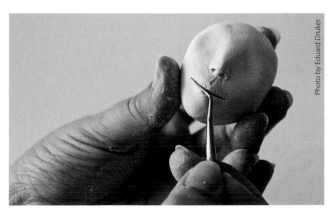

Form the lips.

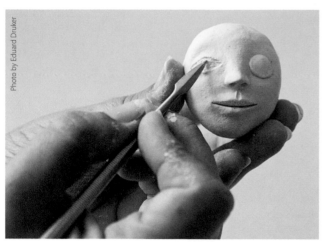

Shape the eyes.

6. For the eyes, add 2 flattened pieces of modeling material, each approximately ½″ wide, over the eye sockets. Smooth and blend them, and then use a flat, pointed tool to contour them and add the suggestion of eyelids. You will add more detail later with paint.

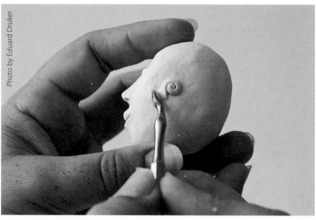

Attach the ears.

7. Add the ears. I always make the ears shaped as small spirals, although you can make a simple ear shape instead if you prefer. I am not striving for realism; and anyway, the ears often end up being hidden under the doll's hair. To make spiral ears, roll out a thin piece, approximately 2″ long, of modeling material and cut it into 2 equal parts. Shape each part into a small spiral and carefully blend the ears into the sides of the head.

The completed and dried head. Note the finished size relative to the size of the original foam base.

8. To complete your doll head, blend all the areas of added modeling material as smoothly as you can. When you are satisfied, set the head aside to thoroughly air dry.

Tip

If your piece develops cracks as it dries, don't despair. Make a paste of water and modeling material, and use it to fill and smooth the cracks. Then allow it to dry thoroughly again.

Making the Hands and Arms

My dolls have two different kinds of hands. One kind (usually for larger dolls) has individual fingers. Because fingers made individually from air-hardening modeling material are very fragile and can easily be broken, I build them on wire frames. The other kind of hand has fingers shaped from one piece of modeling material. For small dolls (especially framed ones), you can sculpt hands as a continuous part of the arm, without the need for wire.

Tip ⌒⌒⌒⌒⌒⌒⌒⌒⌒⌒⌒⌒

When making arms and legs, be sure to make a left and a right, not two lefts or two rights! Always work on both parts of a pair together.

Arms with Wire Frame Hands

1. From 20-gauge craft wire, cut a piece about 7″ long and 5 pieces 1″ long (depending on the size you want your doll to be). The upper part of the wire will be hidden under the clothing, while the arm and hand that will be visible when the doll is dressed will cover the bottom of the wire. Roll out a cylinder of modeling material to the approximate thickness you want the doll's arm to be. Shape the cylinder so it tapers toward the wrist. The cylinder should be slightly longer than the part of the arm that will be visible. Add a flattened piece of modeling material for the palm.

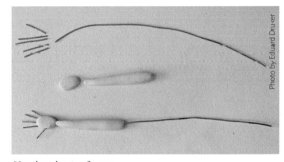
Hand with wire fingers

2. Join the arm and palm by forming the wrist, pushing the arm wire through the arm cylinder and into the palm. Stick the 5 wire pieces into the palm. Cut the ends of the wires to slightly different lengths for the ring finger, index finger, thumb, and so forth. (Check your own hand for comparison.) If you want to make bent fingers, bend the wires before you stick them into the palm. Set aside to air dry.

3. To finish the fingers, you will "paint" them with layers of modeling material. This is a time-consuming process, but it will create very strong fingers. Make a paste of modeling material and water by cutting the material into small pieces, adding some water, and mixing thoroughly. The paste should be soft, similar to toothpaste. Wrap the paste with plastic food wrap to keep it from drying out. Using a thin synthetic brush, apply a layer of the paste to each finger. After the first layer is completely dry, apply the second layer. Continue adding layers; usually it takes 5 or 6 layers to build up the fingers to the desired thickness.

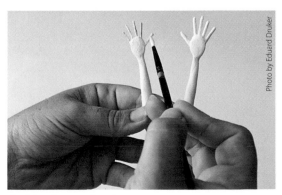
Applying the paste

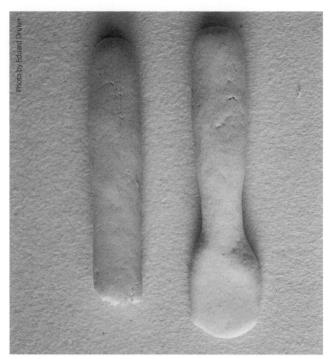

Roughly shaped hand

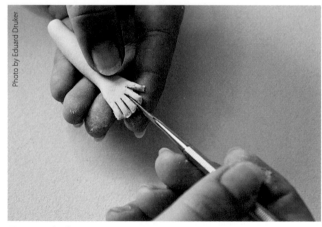

Forming the fingers

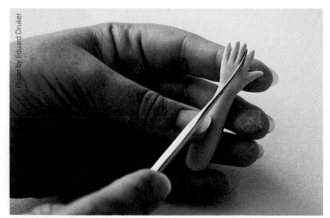

Finishing the fingers

Arms with Sculpted Hands

1. Roll out a cylinder of modeling material to approximately the width you want the doll's arm and hand to be. Press down on the end to create the flat hand area, and roughly shape the flattened area into a hand, trimming as necessary. Shape the arm so it tapers toward the wrist.

2. With the sharp end of a sculpting tool or a fine-bladed knife, cut 4 slices to form the fingers; 3 slices should be of equal length, and the 4 resulting fingers should each be approximately the same width. The fourth slice separates the thumb from the hand; this should be a slightly longer cut that splits off a thicker section.

3. Shape each finger using the round, sharp end of a sculpting tool or a rounded toothpick. Trim the ends of the fingers to create slightly different lengths for the ring finger, index finger, thumb, and so forth. Round off the fingertips, and smooth between and around the fingers. Check the thumb position. You can bend the fingers slightly, but do it very gently and carefully.

4. Cut a piece of 20-gauge craft wire 7″ long and push it through the arm cylinder and a little into the palm.

Making the Legs and Feet

Doll legs and feet are made in different ways for the different dolls in this book. One doll is on a stand, another is freestanding, and another is mounted in a frame; these differences affect the way you use the wire framework and mold the pieces. Refer to the individual projects for instructions.

Finishing the Doll

When you have finished sculpting the doll and the parts are completely dry, you are ready to sand the parts and then do the painting, which will really shape the doll's look and personality.

Sanding

Sanding takes a lot of time, but it is a crucial step before you can begin painting the doll. When you are sure the doll parts are completely dry, use coarse-grained sandpaper to smooth out rough irregularities, filing down the entire surface. (At this stage, there is a lot of dust.) Next, gently use fine-grained sandpaper to achieve the smoothest possible surface. After the first sanding, I moisten the doll under running water and smooth the whole surface with my fingers. The running water washes away the dust and surface scratches, but it does not damage the facial features. The piece dries very quickly, leaving a slightly textured surface (perfect for painting with pastels); it is then very easy to polish it up to perfect smoothness.

Painting

At the painting stage, the doll comes to life. You can use any type of paints listed in Essential Tools and Materials (page 8)—acrylics, watercolors, pastels. You can even use more than one type on the same doll. For example, *Cinderella Princess Doll* (page 27) is tinted with both pastels and acrylics. In this section, you'll find general painting tips; details and variations are presented in individual projects. Work with good lighting, and let each coat dry before applying the next. You may find it helpful to poke a small hole in the molded parts (where they will be connected with wires) and prop the painted pieces up on sticks to dry. Notice in some of the photos in this chapter, I've used a modeling tool to hold the head as it is sculpted and painted.

Always begin by applying a basic allover skin tone on the head, arms, and legs. You can get different effects depending on what mediums you use. One choice is to use acrylic paints, diluted with some water. (These paints are fast-drying, so keep that in mind as you paint.) Use a wide brush to lay down the color in a smooth coat. Usually you will need two or three coats. Another option is to use pastels, applied with a soft sponge.

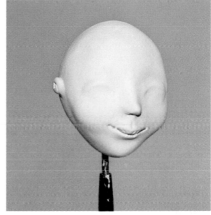

The skin color on Rose Fairy Doll *(page 35) was brushed on with subtly hued acrylic paint.*

On Cinderella Princess Doll *(page 27), the skin color was sponged on with pastels.*

On the face, use paint in a little darker skin tone to add some shading around the nostrils, ears, lips, and eyelids. Apply a blush on the cheeks and chin using either pink-toned acrylic paint or soft pink pastel. Using a fine liner brush, paint the doll's lips with acrylic or watercolor paint. For fingernails and toenails, generally use the same color as the lips.

To paint the eyes, fill in the whites with acrylic paint. Then use a fine liner brush to paint the pupils and add the eyebrows. Keep in mind the following tips when painting.

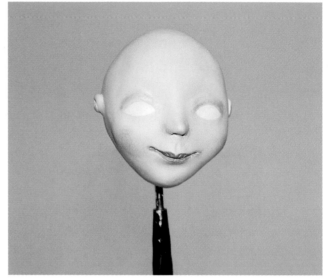

Acrylic paints add cheek and lip color to Rose Fairy Doll *(page 35).*

* The colored iris is always a little hidden by the upper eyelid. Round, wide-open eyes look bulging and unnatural.

* The pupil is always located in the center of the iris, regardless of the direction of the gaze. Usually it is one-third the size of the iris.

* A brown iris often turns out too dark and merges with the pupil.

* Adding tiny white highlights immediately makes the eyes look more alive. White highlight dots should be on the same side of both eyes.

* Use a colored pencil to paint thin lines and a suggestion of eyelashes around the eyes.

* Different eyebrow positions and shapes really affect facial expression. Practice drawing shapes on paper before adding eyebrows on the doll with paint or colored pencil.

Finished head for Rose Fairy Doll

When you are satisfied with your painting, seal all painted areas with a matte protective varnish. If you wish, add a glossy varnish on the eyes and lips to make them shine.

Crazy Quilting
Doll Costumes and Soft Sculptures

My dolls are costumed in lavish, colorful, crazy-quilted clothing made from scraps of silk, velvet, cotton, and other fabrics and embellished with embroidery, lace, ribbon, beads, and charms. My soft sculptures are also created from crazy-quilted fabric.

Crazy quilting is a technique for creating patchwork from random-shaped pieces of various fabrics stitched to a foundation and decorated with embroidery and a lot of embellishments. The technique is often used to make quilts as well as decorative pillows, bags, and even clothing.

Every crazy quilt piece is a unique, one-of-a-kind work of art; there are no rules. You can try to replicate someone else's work, but the result will always be your own.

One of the pleasures of this form of quilting is that you can combine all types of needlework techniques. You can experiment with appliqué, embroidery, and beading all in one project.

The choice of fabrics, colors, and embellishments can convey a doll's theme, mood, and style. For example, the crazy-quilted gown on *Cinderella Princess Doll* (page 27) tells the character's story with humble fabrics and embellishments on the "servant" half and silks, satins, and beads on the "royal" half. *Mermaid on a Patchwork Sea* (page 41) has a crazy-quilted background that includes fabrics in all shades of aquamarine as well as ornaments in the form of fish and small shells. You can create a design in any theme, from music to nature, with your own choices.

Spring, *from the Seasons Collection,*
designed and made by Marina Druker

Fabrics

Crazy quilting makes use of a wide
variety of fabrics, including cotton, silk,
guipure (lace fabric), satin, velvet, and
many others—in almost all the colors of
the rainbow. For these small projects, you
don't need a lot of any one fabric—just
scraps. (A doll dress may turn out to be
no bigger than palm sized!)

Collect as many different kinds of fabric
scraps and trims as you can find. In fabric
and quilt shops, look for remnants, closeout
fabrics, and scrap bags. You can find great
fabrics, yarns, and embellishments at
garage sales and flea markets. And don't
hesitate to ask friends and family members; perhaps they have a forgotten bag of
needlework or other fabric treasure stored
away in an attic or box. Even the tiniest
piece of lace or fabric is useful.

The Internet can be another helpful fabric
source. On quilting forums, members
often share materials. Many forums are
international, giving you an opportu-
nity to get scraps of fabrics or lace from
faraway countries.

In my opinion, the very best way to
build your own fabric stash is to become
acquainted with a dressmaker in your area.
Dressmaking and alteration studios often
throw away small fabric remnants that are
ideal for crazy quilting.

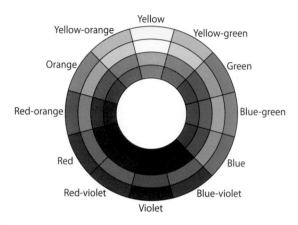

Color

Look at a color wheel to get ideas for combining fabric colors. Simple
color schemes generally work best for the small-scale projects in this
book. The following tips will help you make color choices.

* Working in monochrome can be a very successful approach.
  Choosing one basic color for a doll and then selecting different
  tints, shades, and tones of this color creates a gently blended look,
  without sharp contrasts or bright accents.

* Simple complementary color schemes that use opposites on the
  color wheel can work well for small projects. For example, for my
  doll *Spring* (above), I chose fabric in pale green and pink hues.

* Any three colors located close together on the color wheel—such
  as red, orange, and yellow, or blue, blue-green, and green—are
  analogous colors. These always work well together. Choose one
  color to dominate and a second to support. Use the third color as
  an accent.

* Nature provides perfect examples of harmonious color combinations. Think of flowering plants; the green hues of their foliage
  combine well with almost any color (green and pink, green and
  yellow, green and blue).

* You can combine any color successfully with white or gray.

Texture and Weight

You can achieve interesting visual effects by combining fabrics that have various textures. Solid fabrics can be shiny or matte, textured or smooth. Print fabrics are available in countless designs (florals, stripes, dots) and can vary greatly in the spacing and scale of the motifs.

As you piece together your scraps, try to achieve a balance between solid and print fabrics. If adjacent fabrics are too similar, the piece will look boring. On the other hand, if you use too many print fabrics together, the embroidery and embellishments will be lost on the busy background.

Do make sure that all of your scraps for one project are of the same general weight and thickness. For example, avoid combining fabrics like thick wool and thin natural silk. If fabrics are a little different in weight, you can add thickness to the thin fabric by fusing it to interfacing before sewing it into your patchwork. Not all fabrics are suitable for crazy quilting; unsuitable ones include some types of stretch fabric, fabric with a long nap, and leather.

Embellishments

You can use all kinds of beautiful laces, ribbons, beads, buttons, and charms to embellish the surface of your one-of-a-kind crazy quilting. A wide variety of embellishments gives your crazy quilt originality. There is no right or wrong way to use them. Like fabrics, you can collect them from many sources.

Laces, Trims, and Ribbons

Remnants of trims, ribbons, and lace are often sold at a discount in fabric stores. You can even save the ribbons that decorate gift boxes you receive.

White cotton crocheted lace is very useful because it is so versatile; you can dye and even paint it. Dyeing it with synthetic dyes usually yields bright, clear colors. For delicate shades, you can soak a lace strip for half an hour in a strong solution of tea, coffee, or water tinted with watercolor paint; then rinse and dry.

Don't forget knitting yarns for embellishments. These come in a wide variety of textures and colors, and they are suitable for doll hair as well as for costume decoration.

Pink fabrics in a variety of textures and prints

Lace, ribbons, yarn, and trims are available in endless variety.

Beads, Buttons, and Charms

Beads come in all shapes (round, flat, teardrop, elongated) and are manufactured from different materials (glass, stone, wood, plastic, pearl, and ceramics). Tiny glass seed beads make lovely accents when stitched into your embroidery. Large beads can be the focal point of a design.

Buttons also come in an almost endless variety of colors, shapes, and sizes. Buttons can be grouped on your crazy quilting, set in rows, or even added as the middle of a flower.

Sort your beads and buttons by color and store them in compartmented plastic boxes so you can see them at a glance.

A large selection of metal charms is a great resource for decorating your crazy quilting. You can find silver-plated, brass, copper, and gold-plated charms. Sort them by themes: sea (fish, shells, sea horses), insects (butterflies, dragonflies, bees), animals (cats, elephants, rabbits), flowers and leaves, keys, hearts, and so forth.

Different kinds of embellishments

How to Crazy Quilt

Crazy quilting involves sewing irregularly shaped pieces of fabric onto a foundation. For the foundation, I use fusible interfacing—a woven or nonwoven material that can be ironed to the main fabric to give it support. Interfacings come in a variety of weights to suit different purposes; I use nonwoven featherweight interfacing, which is flexible but sturdy and is heat-activated on one side. I prefer white because you'll be able to see the pencil marks you'll need to make for sewing. (These marks will be hidden once the fabric scraps are sewn on.)

> **Note:** *Although I have provided patterns for the doll clothes, each handmade doll has its own unique size and proportions, so you will need to adjust the pattern to fit your own doll. The patterns are basic guides for you to work from. I recommend using the provided template patterns to make a pattern from a paper towel. Pin the paper towel pattern to the doll and check to see if it needs to be adjusted in length or width. Redraw the pattern if necessary. You may have to repeat this process a couple times. Once the paper towel pattern fits your doll, use it as a template to cut the fabric, adding seam allowances.*
>
> *Because the crazy-quilted fabric gets quite stiff due to its several layers of interfacing, fabric, and decorative embroidery, the shapes of the doll costumes are very simple, without folds or draping, and the pieces for the soft sculptures are simple as well.*

To make a doll costume or soft sculpture, begin by making templates. Depending on the specific project instructions, trace the template patterns provided in this book onto paper or paper towel or onto the interfacing, and cut them out, adding a ¼"–½" seam allowance. Then follow these steps to create the patchwork.

1. Cut out irregularly shaped pieces of your chosen fabrics, and with the adhesive side of the interfacing up, lay them out on the interfacing, moving them around until you like the design. The fabric pieces have to completely cover the interfacing foundation; each scrap should slightly overlap the adjacent pieces. When you are pleased with the layout, follow the interfacing manufacturer's directions to fuse the fabrics to the foundation. Your composition may include fabrics that require different temperatures, such as silk and cotton. If that is the case, protect the fabrics by placing a thin cotton cloth or a pressing sheet over them. For best fusing, apply pressure with your iron and hold for 10–15 seconds each on the right (fabric) side and the wrong (interfacing) side. If some of the fabric edges are still not completely fused, you can tuck in small pieces of ½″ fusible web tape, such as Steam-A-Seam 2 Double Stick.

Fuse the patchwork.

2. Next you must cover the raw edges of the pieces. The seams may be covered with ribbons, lace, or other trims, or they can be embroidered with a combination of stitches (see Embroidery Stitches, page 26). To affix the laces and ribbons, I use textile glue in small quantities. After gluing in place, hand sew each embellishment along its entire length to secure it.

3. Once you have finished the crazy-quilted base, you can give free rein to your fantasies by using all kinds of embellishments. This part is the most fun! Combine everything and anything you love—simple and elaborate embroidery stitches, appliqué, beads, buttons, lace, and charms. When finished with the embroidery, gently iron the crazy quilting piece from the wrong side.

Cover the seams with a variety of ribbons and trims. One seam here is finished with a simple buttonhole (blanket) stitch.

Finished crazy quilting block features embroidered motifs, beading, additional trim, and assorted charms.

embroidery stitches

Some basic embroidery stitches are pictured here. If you are new to embroidery, you can find plenty of books and online sources that will teach you how to do these stitches and many more. Refer to Resources (page 87) for some ideas.

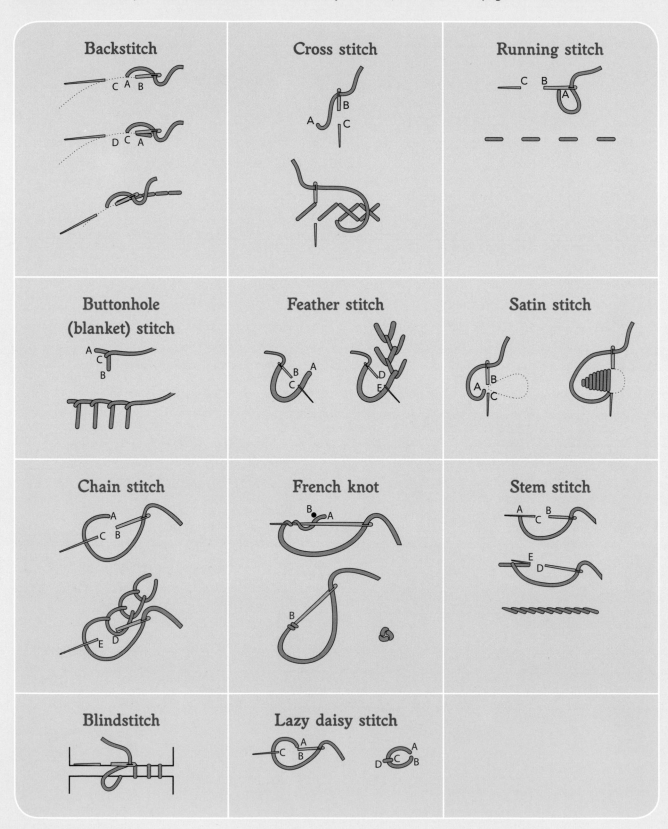

Cinderella Princess Doll

This lovely princess is made from modeling material. Her skirt is crazy quilted from an array of subtle fabric prints in shades of ivory and embellished with lace, trim, and charms. To carry out the Cinderella theme, I designed the doll with two contrasting "halves." One half, dressed in rough fabrics and embellished with charms representing common tools and utensils, is Cinderella the servant, forced to work in her cruel stepmother's home. The other half is Cinderella transformed into a princess, dressed in rich royal fabrics and jewel-like embellishments. Feel free to make your own version of this doll!

Designed and made by Marina Druker

Finished size: Doll 12″ tall; stand 8½″ diameter

materials and supplies

Air-hardening modeling material (4 oz.)

Foam ball 1½" in diameter

Foil

16-gauge craft wire for body frame

20-gauge craft wire for fingers

Chenille stems

Needle-nose pliers

Various sculpting tools

Sandpaper

Soft pastels, watercolor paint, watercolor pencils, and matte acrylic varnish for painting

Sponges, cotton swabs, and fine liner brush for painting

Thin polyester batting

Drinking straws

Thick, soft paper towels for pattern

Wool threads for hair

Doll eyelashes

Textile glue

Superglue

Fusible interfacing 10" × 10", such as Pellon Craft-Fuse iron-on craft backing

Scraps of coordinating prints for the dress bodice, collar, sleeves, and crazy-quilted skirt*

Lightweight fabric ¼ yard for the underwear and the skirt lining

Lace, ribbon, beads, and buttons

Metal charms with royal and kitchen themes (crown, flowers, scissors, spoons, and so forth)

Wood doll stand 7"–8½" in diameter (I stacked 3 round wooden stands, 8½", 6", and 4" in diameter.)

Materials for decorating the stand, such as paint, lace, and varnish

Choose a mix of fabrics—elegant satin and brocade for the royal half of the dress, plain linen and cotton for the servant half.

Instructions

This doll has a head, arms, and legs sculpted from modeling material and a wire body framework secured with chenille stems.

Sculpting the Head, Arms, and Legs

Sculpt the head.

Form the chest with foil over wire.

Sand the head and neck.

1. Sculpt the doll's head but do not paint it yet. For basic modeling steps, refer to Sculpting the Doll (page 12).

2. This doll has a neck and chest formed on a wire frame. After the head has dried, punch a hole in the bottom. Bend a 10" piece of 16-gauge craft wire into an elongated loop. Insert the loop into the head and secure the ends of the wire to the head with superglue. Cover the wire with aluminum foil to form a simple neck and chest shape.

3. Moisten the part of the head that is attached to the neck. Roll out a flat piece of modeling material and apply it over the foil to cover the neck base. Blend the area where the head and neck join. Set the piece aside to dry. When the piece is completely dry, sand it gently with fine sandpaper.

4. Make the arms and hands, referring to the method described in Arms with Wire Frame Hands (page 17). Use 16-gauge wire for the arms and 20-gauge wire for the fingers.

5. Make the legs and feet. This doll is mounted on a stand, so you will need to model the legs on wires that pass through the feet and can be anchored into the stand. For this construction, cut a piece of 16-gauge wire 15" long, and bend it in half.

6. For each leg, form a cylinder of modeling material the approximate thickness you want the doll leg to be. Add another small cylinder of material for the foot, and flatten it to the rough shape of a foot. Pass the wire ends through the 2 legs and feet. You can create a shoe by forming a shoe shape in the heel and the toe area.

7. When the hands and legs are completely dry, sand them gently with fine sandpaper.

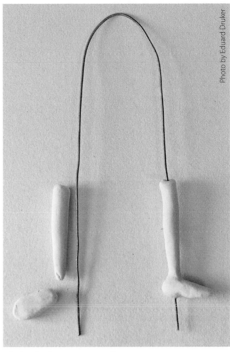

Make the legs on a wire frame.

> **Note:** *For this doll, I chose to add shoes in the form of traditional pointed wooden clogs, to represent Cinderella the servant. I made them out of modeling material and painted them.*

Painting

1. After the sculpting is complete, paint the doll parts. For this doll, I chose soft pastels and water-color pencils. Apply a base coat of skin-tone pastel on the head, hands, and legs using a soft sponge, your fingers, and cotton swabs.

2. Blush the cheeks, chin, and nose area with pink pastel. Paint the whites of the eyes with white acrylic paint using a thin liner brush. Paint the lips with pale red watercolor paint.

Base coat

Paint the eyes and lips.

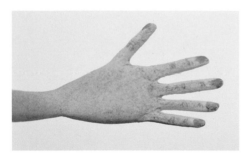

Paint the hands.

Make the torso.

Shape the body.

3. Paint the eyes, adding a dot of black paint for the pupils and a tiny dot of white paint for highlights. Use colored pencil for a lash line and eyebrows.

4. On the hands, use the colored pencil to lightly mark 2 knuckles on each finger. Paint the nails with pale red paint.

> **Note:** *To carry out the Cinderella theme, I smudged one side of the doll's face and one of her hands to suggest the hard-working side of her character.*

5. When the paint is dry, finish with a coat of spray matte acrylic varnish.

Constructing the Body

1. To form the doll's torso, you will need to connect and attach the wire framework you created for the head, arms, and legs. I covered the upper arm wires with short pieces of drinking straws to establish the arm length and give the arms a little more thickness.

2. To attach the arms, pierce a hole in each side of the chest and insert the wires; then glue the ends of the wires.

3. Determine roughly where the waist line will go and wrap the wire ends of the head and legs around each other to create a support for the doll's torso. Use chenille stems to reinforce the connections.

4. To create the body shape, cut the polyester batting into thin strips. Form the body shape by winding the strips around the skeleton. Around the joints, glue the batting to the modeled parts. Affix the ends of the strips with a needle and white thread.

Making the Costume

Template patterns are on pages 78 and 79.

The doll's dress has a crazy-quilted skirt. The bodice and sleeves are each cut from single pieces of fabric. When you make the clothing, use more elegant fabrics for the royal side of the dress and coarser linens and cottons for the servant side. Make the underwear from the lightweight lining fabric. To create a more distressed look for the servant fabrics, you can soak the scraps in coffee and then rinse and dry them. This will also work with cotton lace, as described in Embellishments (page 23).

Remember that all patterns are sized approximately because no two dolls are exactly the same. You will cut out the basic pieces and adjust them on your doll as you go. For the more fitted pieces, you will be instructed to first create a pattern from a paper towel and then adjust the pattern as required. From the fabrics, cut the number of pieces indicated on the pattern, adding a ¼" seam allowance.

Underwear and Sleeves

1. From the lining fabric, cut out pattern piece A for the underwear.

2. To make the underwear, fold each piece A in half lengthwise, right sides together. Stitch from point 1 to point 2. Match the 2 sewn parts, and sew from point 2 to point 3 and from point 2 to point 4. Turn the underwear right side out, and attach it to the doll body with a needle and thread, gathering it to fit at the waistline, the top, and the knees. Stitch the top to create a ruffled appearance. Add lace ruffles around the pantaloon legs. The underwear should completely cover the framework.

3. Cut out the sleeves B, 1 from royal fabric and 1 from servant fabric. Pin the sleeves to the doll, matching the control points. Sew them directly onto the doll from point 1 to point 2, using a blind stitch and turning under the seam allowances. Like the underwear, the dress sleeves must completely cover the framework. Secure the sleeves with textile glue at the joints between the modeling material and the framework.

4. Cut out the sleeve cuffs G, 1 from royal fabric and 1 from servant fabric. Sew strips of lace to the bottom edges of the cuffs, if desired. Baste the cuffs to the bottoms of the sleeves and carefully sew. Decorate the seam with beads.

Tip

You will do a lot of the costume fitting and sewing directly on the doll. To make this easier, set up a temporary doll stand by making a rough cut in a piece of wood and inserting the foot wires into the cut.

Make the underwear and sleeves and attach them to the doll.

Skirt

1. Cut 6 pattern C pieces for the skirt out of paper towel, adding side seam allowances. Baste panels together and, using straight pins, fit and adjust the panels directly on the doll, trimming where necessary. If desired, lengthen the skirt.

2. Remove and smooth out the paper towel patterns; trace around them onto lightweight cardboard and mark the lines for the crazy-quilting patches. Use these modified patterns to cut out 6 pieces of fusible interfacing for the skirt foundation. Select scraps of royal and servant fabrics and follow the drawn lines to arrange them on the foundation. Follow the manufacturer's instructions to fuse them to the interfacing using a hot iron, as described in How to Crazy Quilt (page 24).

Pin and adjust paper towel patterns.

Make the skirt panels.

3. Cover all interior raw edges with lace, trim, or embroidery stitches. For embroidery ideas, see Embroidery Stitches (page 26). Lay 2 skirt panels right sides together, matching points 1 to 3 and 2 to 4, and pin. Machine sew on one side from point 1 to point 2. Add 1 additional panel at a time in the same manner. When you sew on the last panel, leave a side seam open.

4. Embellish the skirt by hand with beads, charms, and buttons. On the servant side, I used charms such as scissors, kitchenware, and a sewing machine, as well as simple wooden beads. For the royal side, I chose embellishments in the form of crowns, butterflies, faux diamonds, and ribbon rosettes.

Servant side of the skirt

Royal side of the skirt

5. Using the modified C templates, cut out 6 skirt pieces from the lining fabric, adding seam allowances, and sew them together as for the outer skirt. Pin decorative trim or a lace ruffle to the hemline of the skirt from Step 4. Lay the outer skirt and lining right sides together, and sew all the way around the hemline. Turn right side out.

6. Sew the skirt to the doll firmly with thread at the waist. Close up the side seam with a blind stitch.

Finished skirt

Bodice and Collar

1. Cut out bodice pieces front D and back E and collar piece F from paper towel. Divide pieces D, E, and F in half vertically. Pin the towel pieces to the doll and adjust the fit and placement, trimming where necessary.

2. Use the adjusted paper towel patterns to cut out pieces D, E, and F from the same fabrics you used for the sleeves, adding seam allowances. Sew them directly onto the doll with a blind stitch, turning under the seam allowances. Use textile glue to further secure the seams. Add lace around the collar and whatever additional embellishments you wish to the dress. I added beads down the bodice front to resemble buttons and beads around the sleeves. To finish the raw edges of the collar and sleeves, I stitched a blanket stitch in matching thread.

Adjust the bodice and collar.

The finished doll head

Finishing the Head

After the clothes are finished, add the hair. This really completes the doll's style. You can choose something close to real hair color (like blond, red, or brown) or a more fanciful color (like pink, blue, or green). I chose soft, curly wool yarn in shades of blond for this doll.

1. You can style and embellish the hair in whatever way you wish. You can braid, curl, cut, roll up, and so forth. Then embellish the hair with strands of beads, ribbons, or whatever you like

To style and embellish the hair as shown, string 2 decorative beads (pearls for the royal side and wood beads for the servant side) on a pin. Make 2. Make 2 holes in the doll's head and glue in the pins. Cut long strands of yarn and use textile glue to affix them to the doll's head, wrapping the strands around the head and around the pins (like "horns"). Then embellish. For the royal half I wound a strand of beads around the hair horn, and for the servant half I used rouge cord. Finally, curl the horns.

2. Very carefully glue on a set of doll eyelashes.

Glue the wire and shoes.

Making the Stand

You can make the stand as fancy or as simple as you wish. I glued together 3 wooden stands of different diameters. I painted the "stairs" in a diamond pattern in bronze and gold and coated them with varnish. I decorated the lower edge with fancy lace trim.

To mount the doll on the stand, mark 2 connection points on the stand and drill small holes. Glue the wire ends that extend beyond the feet into the drilled holes. Glue the bottoms of the shoes to the wooden base.

As a final touch, add some suitable accessories for the doll. I put Cinderella's lost glass slipper on the stairs.

Painted and embellished stand

Rose Fairy Doll

This fanciful fairy is dressed all in pink crazy quilting with a lot of embellishments. She even has fancy shoes on her feet, which are made so that she is freestanding. In her hand she holds a wand, ready to make some magic!

Designed and made by Marina Druker

Finished size: 8½″ tall

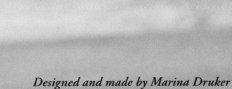

materials and supplies

Air-hardening modeling material (4 oz.)

Foam ball 1½˝ in diameter

Foil

Craft wire (16- and 20-gauge)

Strong thread to secure wires

Chenille stems

Needle-nose pliers

Various sculpting tools

Sandpaper

Acrylic paints, watercolor paints, watercolor pencils, and matte acrylic varnish

Paintbrushes including a wide brush and a fine liner brush

Thin polyester batting

Silk crochet yarn for hair

Doll eyelashes

Textile glue

Superglue

Fusible interfacing 11˝ × 6˝, such as Pellon Craft-Fuse iron-on craft backing

Fusible web 11˝ × 6˝

Scraps of coordinating prints in shades of pink for crazy-quilted dress

Light, gauzy pink fabric 8˝ × 10˝ for underwear and shoes

White ruffled fabric 6˝ × 6˝ for sleeves and pantaloon legs

Lining fabric 6˝ × 12˝ for dress lining

Metallic trim for costume top and hair

Lace, ribbon, beads, buttons, metal charms of fairy themes (flowers, butterflies, etc.) to embellish dress

Light cardstock paper for shoe soles

Wand (see Finishing the Doll, page 40, for instructions to make your own)

Instructions

This doll has a head, arms, and legs sculpted from modeling material. The feet and shoes are also made from modeling material so that the doll is freestanding. The wire body is secured with chenille stems.

Making the Head

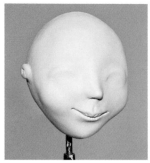

Apply an allover skin tone.

1. Sculpt the doll's head. For basic modeling steps, refer to Sculpting the Doll (page 12). When the head is completely dry, sand it gently with fine sandpaper.

2. Prepare skin-tone paint by diluting acrylic paint with some water. Use a wide brush to lay down the skin-tone color in a smooth coat. Apply the paint in several layers.

Add pink color to the cheeks, eyelids, and lips.

3. Add light pink blush tones on the cheeks, chin, and upper eyelids. Smooth and blend all areas with a dry paintbrush or sponge. Use a fine liner brush to paint the lips with bright pink paint. Paint the whites of the eyes with white acrylic paint.

Finished head

4. Paint the irises of the eyes; add a dot of black paint for the pupils and a tiny dot of white paint for highlights. Use colored pencil to create a lash line and eyebrows. Allow the paint to dry, and finish with a coat of spray matte acrylic varnish.

Making the Arms and Legs

1. This doll has curled fingers on one hand that allow her to hold her wand. Sculpt the hands and arms on a wire frame as described in Arms with Wire Frame Hands (page 17).

2. In order for the doll to stand up without a doll stand, the feet must be extra long for stability. Cut a piece of 16-gauge wire 16″ long for the legs and feet and a piece of 16-gauge wire 12″ long for the legs and shoe heels. Bend both wires as shown to create curves for the legs and feet, and secure them together with a strong thread such as crochet thread.

3. The wire must pass through the legs and the feet. Roll out 2 cylinders of modeling material the approximate thickness you want the doll's legs to be. Add a long cone of the material for making each shoe. Mold the basic leg and shoe shape around the wire.

4. When the arms and legs are completely dry, sand them gently with fine sandpaper. Paint them using the same skin-tone acrylic paint you used for the head. Paint the nails with red paint. Finish the painting with a coat of spray matte acrylic varnish.

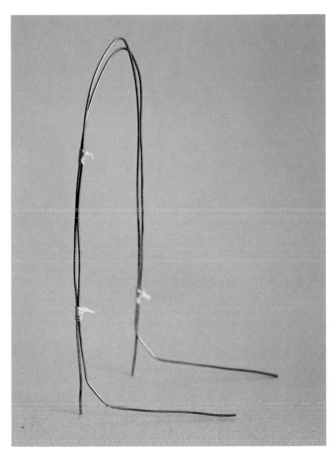

Make a wire frame for the legs and feet.

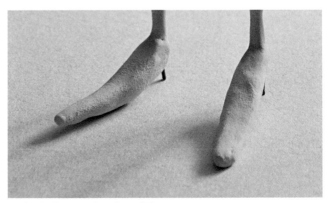

Make the feet extra long for stability.

Constructing the Doll's Body

1. To form the doll's torso, you will need to connect and attach the wires you used for the head, arms, and legs. Measure the wire for the hands and legs according to the proportions of the doll based on the head size and the eventual height you want for the doll.

2. Punch a hole in the bottom of the head. Bend a 10″ piece of 16-gauge craft wire into an elongated loop. Insert the wire ends into the head and secure them with glue.

3. Wrap the wires from the head, arms, and legs around each other to create a support for the doll's torso. Wrap chenille stems around the wire and use them to reinforce the connections as shown in the photo.

4. To create the body shape, cut polyester batting into thin strips. Form the body shape by winding the strips around the skeleton. Around the joints, glue the batting to the modeled parts. Affix the ends of the strips with a needle and white thread. For an example of wrapping the batting around the doll framework, see the bottom photo on page 30.

Making the Costume

Template patterns are on pages 80 and 81.

This fairy doll has a two-piece set of underwear and a dress with a simple shape, crazy quilted from an assortment of pink fabrics and embellished with a lot of trim, buttons, and beads.

> **Note:** *Remember that all patterns are sized approximately because no two dolls are exactly the same. You will cut out the basic pieces from paper towels and adjust them on your doll as you go. From the fabric, cut the number of pieces indicated on each pattern, adding a ¼″ seam allowance.*

Underwear and Sleeves

1. From the white ruffled fabric, cut pieces A and C, lining up the lower edge of the ruffle with the bottom edge of each pattern piece.

2. From the thin, gauzy fabric scraps, cut pieces B. I used 2 different color fabrics, but you can use just 1 if you wish.

3. To make the underwear legs, fold each piece A in half, right sides together, and stitch the seam. Turn the pieces right side out, put them on the doll, and sew them to the body with a needle and thread. Fold each piece B in half,

Tip

To achieve stability for this free-standing doll, bend and adjust the body framework until it balances. I find that making the doll heavier in the pelvis area provides additional stability, shifting the center of gravity down. To do this, I insert a large glass or metal bead within the framework.

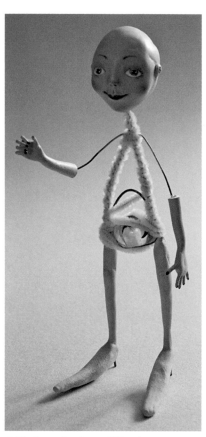

Add a heavy bead to stabilize the doll body framework.

right sides together, and stitch the back seam. Turn these pieces right side out and attach them to the doll body, gathering 1 piece at the legs and waist and the other at the neck and waist.

4. Pin the sleeves C to the doll, matching the control points, and sew them directly on the doll from point 1 to point 2, using a blind stitch and folding under the seam allowances. Secure the sleeves with textile glue at the joints between the modeling material and the framework.

5. Tightly wrap the doll's neck and shoulders with metallic trim, completely covering the body framework.

Dress

1. Place the doll on a sheet of paper and draw a dress outline that approximates the shape of pattern piece D. Cut out this paper dress pattern. Cut 2 pieces D from the fusible interfacing and 2 pieces D from the lining fabric, adding at least ½" seam allowances.

2. Place scraps of various pink fabrics in random order on the 2 pieces of interfacing. Follow the manufacturer's instructions to fuse the fabrics to the interfacing using a hot iron.

3. Embellish the crazy-quilted dress pieces by hand with ribbons, lace, beads, and charms (see Embellishments, page 23).

4. Using fusible web with a hot iron, follow the manufacturer's instructions to fuse the lining pieces to the wrong side of the crazy-quilted pieces. Decorate the hemline with tightly spaced buttonhole (blanket) stitches (see Embroidery Stitches, page 26) and add fancy trim around the dress hemline.

5. Pin the dress pieces on the doll to determine the depth of the armholes. Take them off the doll and place the dress pieces together, with the lining sides facing, and sew together by hand along 1 side, using a buttonhole stitch. Stitch just up to the armhole. Affix the dress to the doll with pins, and carefully sew the other side seam and the shoulder seams.

Attach the underwear sleeves, and wrap metallic trim around the neck and shoulders.

Make and embellish the dress.

Make and attach the shoes.

Shoes

1. Trace and cut out paper patterns E, F, and G. Adjust the patterns, if necessary, to fit your doll. Use these patterns to cut out pieces E and F from the same lightweight pink fabric used for the under- wear. Cut out 2 pieces G from a light cardstock paper, without seam allowances. Cut out 2 pieces G from lightweight pink fabric, adding seam allowances.

2. Use textile glue to attach pieces E to the feet. Glue on pieces F, tucking the fabric edges under the feet. Wrap the fabric G pieces around the cardstock G pieces, and then glue them onto the soles of the feet. Make bows from ribbon and add charms or beads to the centers; attach them at the ankles. String some beads on the heel wires, and affix them with glue.

Finishing the Doll

1. To make the hair, wrap the silk yarn around your fingers 15–20 times, depending on the thickness of the yarn. Slip the yarn off your fingers. Glue the middle of the yarn loop to the top and back of the head using textile glue. Wrap the ends of the hair with metallic thread to make pigtails, or style the hair in whatever way you wish.

2. Very carefully glue on the eyelashes.

3. As a final touch, add a wand in the fairy's hand. I made a wand by painting a toothpick with silver paint and gluing on a star charm.

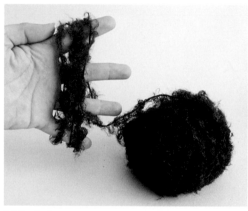

Make the hair.

Mermaid on a Patchwork Sea

This fantasy mermaid doll swims on a crazy-quilted sea at sunrise, within a decorative frame that carries out the nautical theme. She is made entirely from modeling material, sculpted and painted. The background seascape is made from decorative fabrics in pale pink and aqua blue and embellished with trims, beads, embroidery, and a treasure chest of sea-themed charms. The frame is crackle painted to achieve a rustic finish.

Designed and made by Marina Druker

Finished size: Doll 6″ long; frame 12″ × 12″

materials and supplies

Air-hardening modeling material (4 oz.)

Foil

20-gauge craft wire

Needle-nose pliers

Various sculpting tools

Sandpaper

Acrylic paint and matte acrylic varnish for painting doll and frame

Paintbrushes, medium and fine

Wool yarn for hair

Textile glue

Fusible interfacing 12″ × 12″, such as Pellon Craft-Fuse iron-on craft backing

Scraps of coordinating prints in pale pink and blue-green for crazy quilting

Lace, ribbon, beads, buttons, and metal charms with sea themes

2 metal bead cups

Frame 12″ × 12″

Crackling medium for frame

Instructions

This mermaid is made of modeling material on a wire and foil base, and painted using acrylic paints. The background is crazy quilted and applied to the frame before mounting the mermaid over it.

Making the Mermaid

When you create the mermaid, keep in mind the size of the frame in which you will place her. She should be neither so large that she dominates the background seascape nor so small that she is lost in it.

Head and Body

1. Cut a piece of 20-gauge craft wire 5″ long and bend it into an arc. From the foil, form a rough shape around the wire for the mermaid head, trunk, and tail. Keep in mind that the completed form will be about a third larger than the base when you add layers of modeling material.

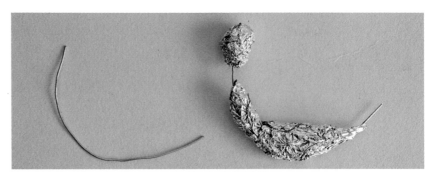

Bend the wire and make a basic foil shape.

2. Referring to Sculpting the Doll (page 12), cover the base with modeling material to about ¼″ thick, pressing it onto the base. Moisten and add small pieces to the face for modeling the features. The mermaid's head has a very simple shape, without sockets for the eyes. Form the trunk and tail. Set the mermaid aside to air dry.

Sculpt the mermaid head, body, and tail, and then add the wire frame for the arms.

3. Pierce holes in the shoulders. Cut a piece of 20-gauge craft wire 4½″ long, and insert the wire into the trunk for the arms, bending them to a pleasing shape.

4. Moisten the top of the torso and form the neck from a small piece of modeling material.

Completed mermaid form

5. Moisten the portion of the trunk where the arms will be added, and roll out thin cylinders of modeling material the approximate thickness of the doll's hand. Refer to Arms with Sculpted Hands (page 18) to sculpt the arms and hands.

6. When the mermaid is completely dry, sand the entire surface gently with fine sandpaper.

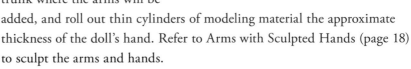

Painting and Finishing

1. For this doll I chose all acrylic paints—skin tone for the head and torso, and aqua blue with silver accents for the tail. Referring to Painting (page 19) for general instructions, lay down a base coat of skin tone on the head, hands, and torso. Let paint dry. Lay down an aqua blue coat on the tail. Apply the paint in 2 or 3 layers, allowing it to dry between layers.

2. Once the base is dry, add pink blush to the cheeks, and paint the whites of the eyes white. Paint the lips with bright red acrylic paint.

3. Use a thin brush to paint the irises of the eyes with aqua blue; add a dot of black paint for pupils and a tiny dot of white for highlights. Use the same aqua blue acrylic paint for lash lines and eyebrows.

4. Use a fine brush to add scales to the tail with silver acrylic paint.

5. Finish with a coat of spray matte acrylic varnish.

6. Cut long strands of curly wool yarn and glue them onto the head using textile glue. I styled the long hair into an updo, but you can style it in whatever way you like.

7. Pierce 2 holes all the way through the mermaid's chest. Attach metal bead cups with long pins. Don't cut the ends of the pins; you will use them to attach the mermaid to the background board.

Paint the face, torso, and tail.

Completed mermaid

Crazy Quilting the Background Seascape

1. On a 12″ × 12″ piece of paper, draw a simple sunrise sketch. Draw lines inside the square to allow for the frame.

2. Cut a square 12″ × 12″ from fusible interfacing. Referring to your pattern, compose the sky from scraps of pink fabric arranged like rays of the sun on the piece of interfacing. Place scraps of green and blue fabrics in random order on the bottom area of the interfacing for the sea. Follow the manufacturer's instructions to fuse the fabrics to the interfacing using a hot iron.

3. Embellish the background seascape by hand with trims, ribbons, beads, and buttons, as well as embroidery stitches. Charms with sea themes abound—fish, sea horses, boats, shells, pieces of mother-of-pearl, and glass beads are just a few examples.

Sketch a sunrise design.

Tip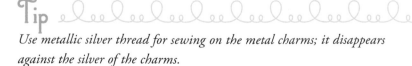

Use metallic silver thread for sewing on the metal charms; it disappears against the silver of the charms.

Fuse the scraps to the interfacing.

Frame with crackle finish

Decorating the Frame

For the frame decoration I chose to use a crackle painting technique, which produces a finish that looks like old cracked paint with older layers of paint showing through. For this technique, you need two different colors—one for the undercoat, and one for the topcoat. I used aqua blue and ivory. Alternatively, you can just paint the frame a single color.

1. Paint the frame with acrylic aqua blue paint using a wide brush. This is the undercoat that will show through the crackling. Allow it to dry.

2. Apply the crackling medium according to the manufacturer's instructions. Then apply the topcoat of ivory acrylic paint. Allow to dry completely.

Attach the mermaid.

Assembling the Project

1. Gently press the background crazy quilting piece from the wrong side.

2. Cut a square of cardboard to fit inside the frame. Carefully glue the crazy-quilted background onto the cardboard.

3. Join the frame and the background piece.

4. Poke 2 holes through the backboard where you want to place the mermaid. Attach the mermaid using the ends of the pins you put in the mermaid's torso.

5. As a final touch, I glued some embellishments onto the frame. I added a small sailboat made of wood and fabric, with an anchor charm on a chain.

Butterfly Doll in a Frame

A little butterfly flits across this decorative panel on wings of gauzy white. The doll is made from modeling material on a wire framework, and her simple costume is crazy quilted. This framed doll would be a wonderful gift.

Designed and made by Marina Druker

Finished size: Doll 7″ tall; frame 7″ × 7″

materials and supplies

Air-hardening modeling material (4 oz.)

Foil

20-gauge wire

Chenille stems

Needle-nose pliers

Various sculpting tools

Sandpaper

Acrylic paint, watercolor pencils, matte acrylic varnish for painting

Paintbrushes, including a fine liner brush, and sponges for painting

Textile glue

Superglue

Fusible interfacing 7″ × 4″, such as Pellon Craft-Fuse iron-on craft backing

Scraps of coordinating green prints for crazy quilting

White fabric 6″ × 6″ for wings

Lining fabric 4″ × 4″ for dress

White chenille yarn for arms, legs, and hair

Lace, ribbon, beads, buttons, and metal charms

2 pins for antennae

Waxed dental floss

White frame 7″ × 7″

Decorative floral paper for background

Butterfly stickers or prints of butterflies for decorating frame

Instructions

The butterfly doll has a crazy-quilted dress and is mounted on a white frame.

Making the Butterfly Doll

This doll's head, hands, and legs with bare feet are sculpted from modeling material; her wire body is secured with chenille stems.

Head and Body

1. Sculpt the doll's head. For basic modeling steps, refer to Sculpting the Doll (page 12). Set the head aside to dry.

2. On this doll, the hands are sculpted on all-wire arms. Cut and bend a piece of 20-gauge wire for the arms. Referring to Arms with Sculpted Hands (page 18), roll out small pieces of modeling material for the hands, shape them around the wire ends, and create fingers.

3. To make the legs and feet, cut 2 pieces of 20-gauge wire. Roll out 2 cylinders of modeling material in the approximate thickness you want the legs to be. Sculpt legs that are bent at the knees. For the bare feet, shape the foot roughly, round off the heels, and press down on the foot front to make this area flat. If you want to suggest toes, use the sharp end of a sculpting tool to cut 4 lines to form the toes, with the big toe wider than the others. Form the arch. The toe area is always slightly wider than the arch and heel area of the foot. Check your own foot for reference.

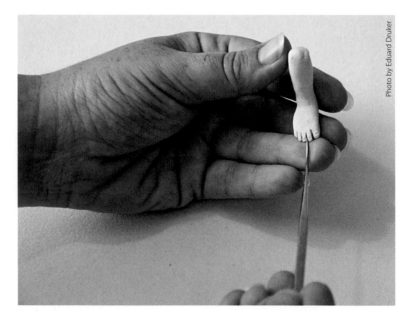

Sculpt the toes.

4. When all the parts are completely dry, sand them gently with fine sandpaper.

5. Prepare skin-tone paint, diluting acrylic paint with some water. Use a wide brush to lay down the skin tone in a smooth coat on the head and all the parts. Apply the paint in several layers.

6. Add light pink blush tones on the cheeks, chin, and upper eyelids. Smooth and blend all areas with a dry paintbrush or sponge. Use a fine liner brush to paint the lips with bright pink paint. Paint the whites of the eyes with white acrylic paint.

7. Paint the irises of the eyes; add a dot of black paint for the pupils and a tiny dot of white paint for highlights. Use colored pencil to create a lash line and eyebrows.

8. Add pink accents on the knees and toenails.

9. After the paint has dried, finish all the parts with a coat of spray matte acrylic varnish.

10. Poke a hole in the underside of the doll's head for the neck, and insert 2 chenille stems. Secure in place with superglue.

11. To form the torso, measure the wire for the arms and legs according to the proportions of the doll. Wire the legs together and connect the head, hand, and leg wires by adding chenille stems to create the body framework.

12. Cut polyester batting into thin strips. Form the body shape by winding the strips around the skeleton (see bottom photo on page 30). Around the joints, use textile glue to attach the batting to the modeled parts. Secure the ends of the strips with a needle and white thread. Tightly wrap the hands, legs, and neck with white chenille yarn. Secure the ends with white thread.

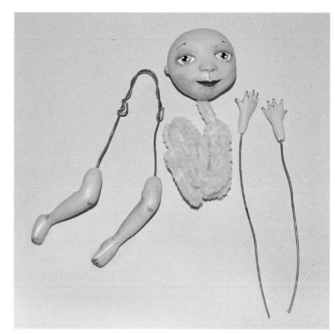

Completed parts of the doll

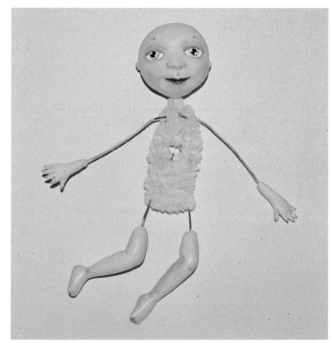

Make the doll frame.

Costume

Template patterns are on page 82.

Remember that all patterns are approximately sized because no two dolls are exactly the same. You will cut out the basic pieces and adjust them on your doll as you go. From the fabric, cut the number of pieces indicated on the pattern, adding a seam allowance.

1. Place the doll onto a sheet of paper and draw a sleeveless dress outline that approximates the shape of pattern piece A. Cut out this paper dress pattern. Cut a piece A from the fusible interfacing and a piece A from the lining fabric, adding at least ½″ seam allowances to each piece. Since the doll will be attached to the frame, you will need only the front of the dress.

2. Place scraps of various green fabrics on the piece of interfacing. With a hot iron, fuse them to the interfacing. Embellish the crazy-quilted dress by hand with ribbons, trim, and beads.

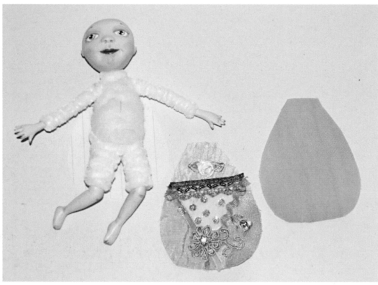

Make the dress.

3. Place the embellished and lining parts right sides together. Sew from point 1 to point 2, leaving the leg spaces open. Turn right side out.

4. Place the dress on the doll as desired and hold in place with pins. Hand sew the dress directly to the doll's body using green thread.

Completing the Doll

1. To make the butterfly antennae, string tiny green beads on pins and bend them. Make 2 holes in the doll's head and glue the antennae in place with superglue.

2. Cut long strands of white chenille yarn. Wind them around the head and the antennae to form the hair, and glue in place with textile glue.

3. Carefully glue on the doll eyelashes.

4. Cut out wing parts B and C from the white fabric, and seal the raw edges with textile glue. Hand sew the wings to the doll's back.

Attach the doll with dental floss.

Assembling the Project

1. To decorate the frame, use butterfly stickers or cut out butterflies from printed paper and glue them on with textile glue or any glue that dries clear.

2. Cut out a piece of decorative paper with a floral theme to fit the inside the frame. Glue the background to the frame with superglue.

3. Cut 3 long pieces of dental floss. Using a needle, anchor the dental floss to the doll's back in 3 places. Poke holes through the backboard and insert the floss. Tie it in firm knots to anchor it to the background; you can also use glue for extra security.

Brooch Doll Trio

These fun and quirky pendant brooch dolls have faces made from covered buttons, and arms and legs made from beads and metal charms. Their dresses are very simple pieces of fabric enhanced with embellishments. These dolls make wonderful pins to wear. The metal base of the buttons also allows you to use them as magnets on a refrigerator or other metal surface. And at Christmas time, you can even use them as tree ornaments.

Designed and made by Marina Druker

Finished size: *2″ × 6″*

materials and supplies

These materials will make 1 doll.

Covered button kit (mold and pusher, button to cover size #60 with pin back)*

Superglue (*optional*)

2 silver-plated hand charms

2 silver-plated shoe charms

4 silver-plated eye pins and connector rings for arms and legs

Small chain, 1″ long with 2 connector rings, for neck

Beads for arms and legs

4″ × 4″ template plastic

Small hole punch

Needle-nose pliers

Textile paints, colored pencils, and matte acrylic varnish for painting

Silk or wool yarn

Textile glue

White cotton muslin 3″ × 3″ for face

Scraps of fabric 4″ × 6″ for dress

Lace, ribbon, beads, buttons, and metal charms

*Glue a pin back to the back of the covered button using superglue.

Tip

If you can find a small-scale fabric print featuring a face, you can use it in place of painted muslin for an instant doll face!

Instructions

These little dolls have covered-button heads and simple fabric dresses glued onto a plastic base. The bead arms and legs are strung on eye pins.

Making the Doll Head

The head is made from a covered button, which has a round, slightly convex surface, ideal for a doll head.

1. Cut out a round piece of white cotton muslin about 1″ larger in diameter than the button.

2. Follow the manufacturer's directions to cover the button with the muslin.

3. Sew small pieces of yarn to the cotton base to make the doll's hair.

4. Using the textile paints and colored pencils, paint the eyes, nose, and mouth, and spray the finished button with acrylic varnish to protect the surface. Be sure to test the paint and varnish on a scrap of fabric first; the varnish may cause some paints to fade.

Make the covered button head and plastic body.

Making the Dress

Template pattern is on page 83.

1. Trace dress pattern A, and cut a dress from the template plastic. Punch holes for attaching the legs and neck.

2. For the legs and feet, attach 2 metal shoe charms to eye pins. String large beads on each pin, and make a loop on each pin end. Attach the pins to the plastic dress base using pliers.

3. Glue lace along the hemline of the plastic dress base.

4. Cut 2 pieces A from fabric, adding a ¼″ seam allowance. Because the dress is so small, it's best to use a single type of fabric instead of the multiple fabrics used in most crazy quilting.

5. Embroider decorative stitches over the dress pieces, and add beads and embellishments.

6. Using a buttonhole (blanket) stitch as described in Embroidery Stitches (page 26), sew together the front and back along the side seams. Keep the small top section open for attaching the head. Add a lace ruffle to the hemline of the dress.

Assembling the Parts

1. Using a connector ring, attach a chain to the neck hole on the plastic base. Put the sewn dress on the base, and pass the chain through the open top section. Shorten the chain to the desired length. The chain should reach the metal shank on the back of the button. Between the lower edge of the button and the dress, you will need 1 free link of the chain. Use a connector ring to attach the chain to the button loop (shank).

2. Secure the chain to the bottom of the button at the neck with a needle and thread to prevent the doll's body from swinging too much.

3. To make the arms, attach 2 metal hand charms to eye pins. String small beads on each pin, and make a loop on each pin end. Sew the pins to either side of the dress.

4. Add a flower or a collar of frilled ribbon to the neck area.

Assemble the dress body and head using a chain.

Tack chain to button fabric with stitches.

Secure the chain to the button fabric.

Complete the assembly.

Fantasy Fish

These small fish are simple in shape, but their rich assortment of embellishments gives them their own individual character. Making them is a quick and easy project. You can dangle the finished fish by threads to make a mobile or use them as decorations on a Christmas tree.

Designed and made by Marina Druker

Finished size: 6″ × 2″

Instructions

The template pattern is on page 83.

You can make a fish with the tail as part of the body or add a separate tail made from organza. Add a fin, made either from organza or from lace or other trim. Keep in mind that the finished fish will look smaller than the pattern because it will be stuffed.

1. Trace the pattern for piece A. Cut a piece A and a piece A reversed from colored cotton, adding a ½" seam allowance around both.

2. For the crazy quilting, cut strips of equal width, like those on the pattern, from fabric scraps and from fusible web. On each cotton foundation piece, center the fusible web strips and place the fabric scraps on top. Follow the manufacturer's instructions to fuse the scraps to the cotton using a hot iron.

3. Embroider decorative stitches over the fabric strips. Embellish both pieces of the body by hand with ribbons, lace, and small beads. Do not add metal charms or bulky beads; they will make it hard to turn the fish right side out when you are finished sewing it.

4. Sew on sequins for eyes.

materials and supplies

Makes 1 fish.

Colored cotton 9" × 6" for main body foundation

Scraps of coordinating prints for crazy quilting

Organza for tail and fin (*optional*)

Fusible web 8" × 6"

Lace, ribbon, and beads for fins and embellishments

4 sequins for eyes
(2 medium, 2 small)

Polyester fiberfill

Tip

If you wish, you can make the fish from just one fabric with wide stripes instead of creating sections with crazy quilting.

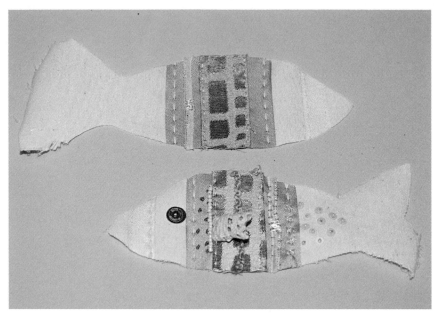

Embellish the fish.

5. Sew on small pieces of lace or other trim for the lateral fins.

6. Sew a small piece of lace or other trim to the top raw edge for the dorsal fin. Make sure it points inward, toward the body.

7. Lay the 2 sides of the body right sides together, aligning the strips. Pin and sew all the way around from point 1 to point 2. Leave an opening at the back to turn and stuff. You can sew by hand or on the sewing machine. Turn the fish right side out.

8. Stuff small bits of polyester fiber-fill into the fish. Close up the back seam with a blind stitch.

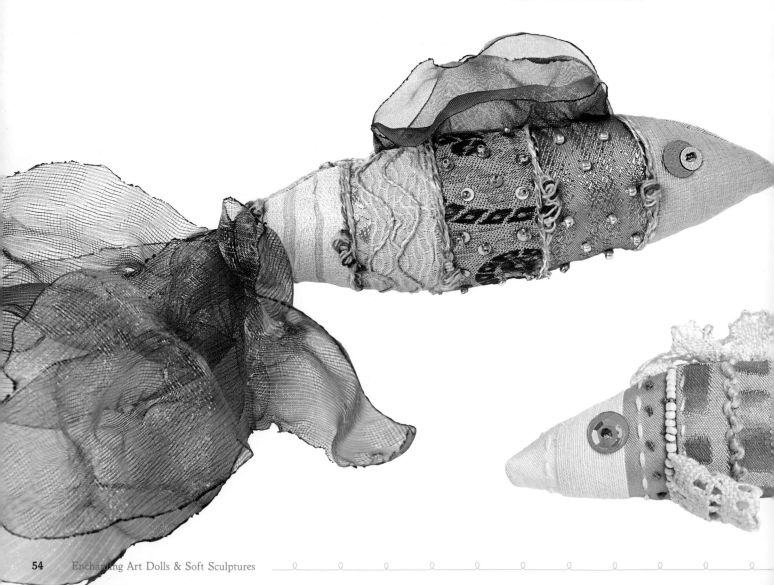

Elegant Teddy Bear

This fanciful little bear is made from soft cotton, print fabrics, and velvet, and embellished with lace, charms, buttons, and beads in a rich patchwork of textures and patterns. I chose fabrics in beige and brown shades with floral motifs for the crazy-quilted sections. The bear is fully jointed.

Designed and made by Marina Druker

Finished size (seated):
6″ wide × 7″ high × 5″ deep

materials and supplies

Light-colored cotton 9″ × 15″
for head and body parts

Scraps of coordinating prints
for crazy quilting

Scraps of velvet for ears and footpads

Fusible interfacing 20″ × 15″, such as
Pellon Craft-Fuse iron-on craft backing

Teddy bear joint set 20mm or 25mm
(up to 1″) (10 hardboard disks; 10 metal
washers; 5 connecting T-pins)*

Set of glass eyes* or large
buttons or beads

Lace, ribbon, beads, buttons,
and metal charms

Cotton crochet thread (black and beige)

Waxed thread for attaching eyes

Polyester fiberfill

Needle-nose pliers

Awl

*Look for teddy bear parts at your local craft
store or online at www.glasseyesonline.com.*

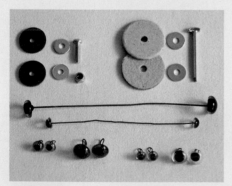

Teddy bear joints and glass eyes

Instructions

Template patterns are on pages 84 and 85.

This teddy bear has a crazy-quilted head, body, outer arms, and outer legs.
His face and his inner arms and legs are made of light-colored cotton, and
his ears and footpads are soft velvet.

Making the Crazy-Quilted Sections

1. Before cutting, fuse the whole piece of light-colored cotton to interfacing
to strengthen the fabric.

2. Cut the following pieces, adding seam allowances to each piece except as
noted. From interfaced cotton, cut a head side piece A, a head side piece A
reversed, an arm piece D, an arm piece D reversed, a leg piece E, and a leg
piece E reversed.

From fusible interfacing, cut a head gusset piece B, a body piece C, a body
piece C reversed, an arm piece D, an arm piece D reversed, a leg piece E,
and a leg piece E reversed. Also cut 2 footpad pieces G without seam
allowances from fusible interfacing.

From velvet fabric, cut 4 ear pieces F. Also cut 2 footpad pieces G without
seam allowances from velvet.

3. Fuse velvet pieces G to fusible interfacing pieces G.

4. Transfer the pattern markings onto the cut cotton pieces. The small
circles indicate where finished body parts will be joined; mark these with a
stitch of contrasting thread. Set aside all cotton and velvet pieces; these will
not be crazy quilted.

5. For the remaining parts,
which will be crazy quilted,
place scraps of coordinating
fabrics in random order on
the pieces of interfacing.
Follow the manufacturer's
instructions to fuse them
to the interfacing using a
hot iron.

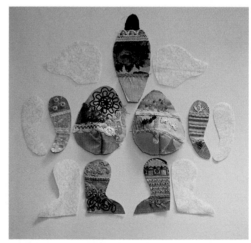

Teddy bear parts, embellished and ready for assembly

6. Embellish the parts by
hand with ribbons, lace,
beads, and buttons. Do not
add beads or other bulky
items close to the joints.

Assembling the Head and Main Body

I prefer to sew these parts together by hand using a backstitch (see Embroidery Stitches, page 26). Backstitches should be small and tight so that parts fit snugly together. You can pin the pieces before sewing.

1. Match 2 head side pieces A right sides together, and sew from point 1 to point 2. Place the head gusset B between the head pieces, and sew on one side from the beginning of the nose (point 1) to the neck (point 3). Then sew the other side in the same fashion from point 1 to point 3.

2. Lay each pair of ears right sides together. Sew from point 4 to point 5 along the curved edge. Turn right side out.

3. On each body piece C, sew a dart from point 6 to point 7. Place the C body pieces right sides together, and sew all the way around from point 8 to point 9. To leave an opening at the neck for the joint, skip a couple of stitches where indicated at the neck, but do not break the thread; continue stitching to point 9. Leave an opening at the back to turn and stuff.

4. Turn the head right side out. Stuff the head with fiberfill, beginning with the nose. Make sure the head and especially the nose are very firmly stuffed.

5. I prefer to embroider the nose and attach the eyes while the neck is still open. Decide what shape you would like for the nose and mouth. Stitch the nose and mouth using black cotton crochet thread. You can make vertical or horizontal satin stitches.

Embroider the nose and mouth.

6. Play with the placement of the glass eyes until you like the way they look. Mark those spots with a pen. Usually glass eyes have a loop for attachment. Carefully poke a small hole in each marked spot with an awl. Insert a long needle and long thread in through the neck and out at the eye hole. Thread the needle through the loop on the glass eye, and insert the needle back into the eye hole, coming down and out at the neck. Pinch the glass eye loop together using pliers. Do the same for the other eye. Pull the thread ends from each eye while gently pushing on the eyes to embed them. Take 1 thread end from each eye and knot it firmly. Repeat with the other 2 thread ends. Bury the ends into the head.

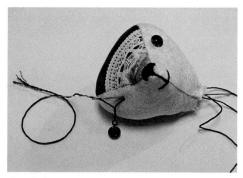

Attach the eyes.

7. Add small bits of stuffing to the neck if needed. Assemble a joint (T-pin, metal washer, and hardboard disk), and set it inside in the neck. Sew the opening with waxed thread to close the neck around the disk, and pull it very tight. Don't stuff the bear's body yet!

8. Sew the ears to the head with a blind stitch, turning the seam allowances to the inside.

Sewing the Arms and Legs

1. The teddy bear arms are rather narrow, so they are sewn together with right sides out. Match the embellished and plain arm pieces D together and trim close to the seamline. Sew on the front side from point 10 to point 11, using a tiny buttonhole (blanket) stitch with beige cotton crochet thread. Refer to Embroidery Stitches (page 26) to see a buttonhole stitch.

2. Sew the leg pieces E in the same way as the arms with cotton crochet thread from point 12 to point 13 and from point 14 to point 15. Insert the velvet footpad G, matching up points 12 and 15, and sew around on the front side.

3. Use a stuffing tool such as a chopstick to carefully and firmly stuff small bits of fiberfill into the arms and legs.

4. Assemble the remaining joint parts, and poke a small hole in the place for each joint with an awl. The disk will be on the inside of each arm and leg.

5. Finish stuffing the arms and legs, and close the seams using the buttonhole stitch.

Assembling the Bear

Now it's time to put all of the bear's parts together. Start with the head.

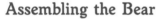
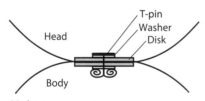

Neck joint construction

1. There is a small gap in the neck seam where the neck joint will fit. Holding the head, slip the T-pin though the neck opening. Reach through the back opening to assemble the second neck disk and second washer over the pin. With needle-nose pliers, carefully bend each side of the pin to join the head to the body. Make it just loose enough that the parts can rotate to turn the head. The joints require a delicate balance: The head or limb has to turn, but it must also be very tightly secured so as not to droop.

2. At the joint markings for the arms and legs, gently poke a small hole with an awl. Attach the arms and legs as you did the head.

3. Stuff the body very tightly. Don't forget to add fiberfill around the joints and at the bear's neck. After finishing filling, close up the back seam with a blind stitch.

Assemble the arms with buttonhole stitches.

Attach the footpad.

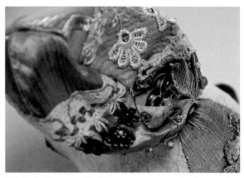

With the bear upside down, you can see the bent ends of the T-pin inside the top of the body.

Add the arms and legs.

Enchanted Cottage

This little fairy-tale house is a perfect "canvas" for creating any kind of theme or mood. You can make it as I made mine—a gingerbread house, with candy motifs in the crazy quilting and embellishments. Or you could make a farmhouse, complete with animal and vegetable charms and countryside colors, or a garden house decorated with floral embroidery and beautiful silk ribbons. The crazy quilting for the roof, gables, and walls is done separately and then applied to a foundation of cardboard.

Designed and made by Marina Druker

Finished size: 3¼" wide × 7" high × 5" deep

Scraps of coordinating prints for crazy quilting (I used light beige and yellow scraps for the walls and windows and red scraps for the tile roof.)

Light-colored cotton 20″ × 20″ for the lining

Fusible interfacing 20″ × 20″, such as Pellon Craft-Fuse iron-on craft backing

Lace, ribbon, beads, buttons, and metal charms

Cotton crochet thread

Waxed thread

Cardboard 20″ × 20″

Instructions

Template patterns are on page 86.

This project is largely made using crazy quilting, so let your imagination go with your use of fabrics, trims, and embellishments.

Making the Roof, Gables, and Walls

1. Trace the template patterns and use them to cut pieces A, B, and C from the lining fabric and interfacing, adding a ½″ seam allowance on all sides. Note that pattern B is for the roof, side walls, and foundation (base). Also cut each piece from the cardboard, without added seam allowances. Transfer the pattern outlines onto the cut-out lining fabric, interfacing, and cardboard pieces.

2. To crazy quilt the walls and gables, arrange scraps of decorative fabric in random order on the interfacing pieces; add rectangles and arch-shaped pieces for windows and doors. For the roof, place rectangular pieces of fabric on the interfacing roof pieces in an arrangement that looks like tiles. Follow the manufacturer's instructions to fuse all the pieces to the interfacing using a hot iron.

3. Generously embellish all the parts by hand with trim, lace, beads, buttons, and charms. Be careful not to place bulky embellishments too close to the edges. Use yarn to embroider the window and door frames.

Embellish the house walls, gables, and roof.

Assembling the House

1. Pair each embellished piece with a piece of lining, right sides together. Pin and machine sew them together on 3 sides (2 sides for the gables). Leave a side open on each piece. Also sew together the 2 foundation pieces in the same manner.

2. Clip the corners diagonally, and turn the pieces right side out so they are like pockets.

3. Insert a cardboard piece into each pocket. Tuck under the seam allowances, and hand sew each piece closed with a blind stitch.

4. Sew together all the walls from the outside, using a buttonhole (blanket) stitch with cotton crochet thread. The project photo (page 59) shows this stitching where the walls meet. Also sew together the 2 halves of the roof. A buttonhole stitch ensures a smooth and stable connection and looks decorative at the same time. Refer to Embroidery Stitches (page 26) to see how to do this stitch.

5. To attach the foundation to the walls, thread a needle with a long piece of waxed thread. Use a loose running stitch to stitch the edges together, passing the needle alternately through the wall and the foundation, leaving loose thread between them along the bottom edge. Use a separate needle and a separate waxed thread for each side of the house.

6. When all walls and the foundation are loosely attached, carefully pull the thread and tighten the stitches until the wall and foundation are securely joined. Tighten the threads and anchor the ends with knots to secure them.

7. Attach the roof to the top edge of one wall with a blind stitch. Now you have a box you can open!

Completed parts of the house

Attach the foundation.

Doll Gallery

Photo by Alexander Kuznetsov

Anastasia Yanovskaya

(Moscow, Russia)

nastini_kukly.livejournal.com

Anastasia Yanovskaya is a master of art dolls. She graduated from the Aerospace University and at the same time studied painting and drawing on wood; she also created theater costumes. She started to make dolls in 2004. She has experimented with many materials, but using Creative Paperclay has helped her find her own style. She has participated in and won many international art doll exhibitions.

Rose Scent, by Anastasia Yanovskaya, 2009
Made from Creative Paperclay

Twilight, *by Anastasia Yanovskaya, 2011*
Made from Artista Formo

Elena Kunina
(Holon, Israel)
www.facebook.com/ekdolls

Elena Kunina earned a master's degree in art history and theory from Moscow State University. A member of the Russian Artists' Union, she is a lecturer and author of the book *Secrets of a Doll Master.* She holds many professional awards, and her dolls are in museums and private collections all over the world. She lives in both Holon, Israel, and Moscow, Russia. The characters she creates are so realistic that viewers sometimes mistake photos of them for those of real people.

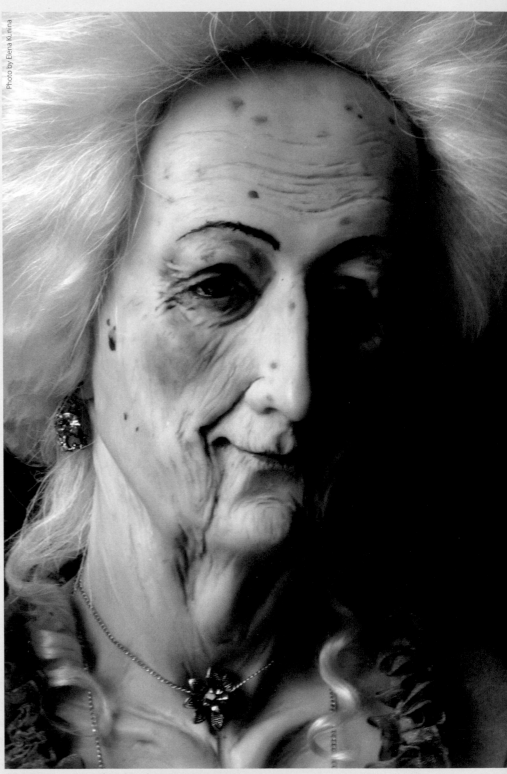

Photo by Elena Kunina

The Queen of Spades, *by Elena Kunina, 2010*
Made from Super Sculpey Living Doll polymer clay

Florence, *by Elena Kunina, 2010*
Made from Super Sculpey Living Doll polymer clay

Svetlana Pekarovsky
(Bat Yam, Israel)
www.svetapek.com

Svetlana Pekarovsky graduated from Kiev State Institute of Arts and Crafts in Ukraine. For many years, she has illustrated children's books and created cartoons. In 1991 she immigrated to Israel, where she now works as an animation designer and illustrator. She started making art dolls in 2007, and currently she fills her free time with painting and with creating dolls.

The Queen of Hearts,
by Svetlana Pekarovsky, 2010
Made from Creative Paperclay

Photo by Svetlana Pekarovsky

Violet, by Svetlana Pekarovsky, 2010
Made from LaDoll

Yulia Litvinova
(St. Petersburg, Russia)
www.dollyland.ru

Yulia Litvinova has been creating dolls since 2008 and takes an active part in international and Russian exhibitions. All her dolls are one-of-a-kind works of art. Most are in private collections; some can be seen in Gallery GLASS and Gallery SUOK in St. Petersburg, Russia. In 2011, Yulia took second place for the Hannie Sarris award from the prestigious competition of DABIDA (the Institute for Dutch and Belgian Doll Art). She makes dolls of papier-mâché and mixed media.

About the Princess,
by Yulia Litvinova, 2009
Made from papier-mâché
and mixed media

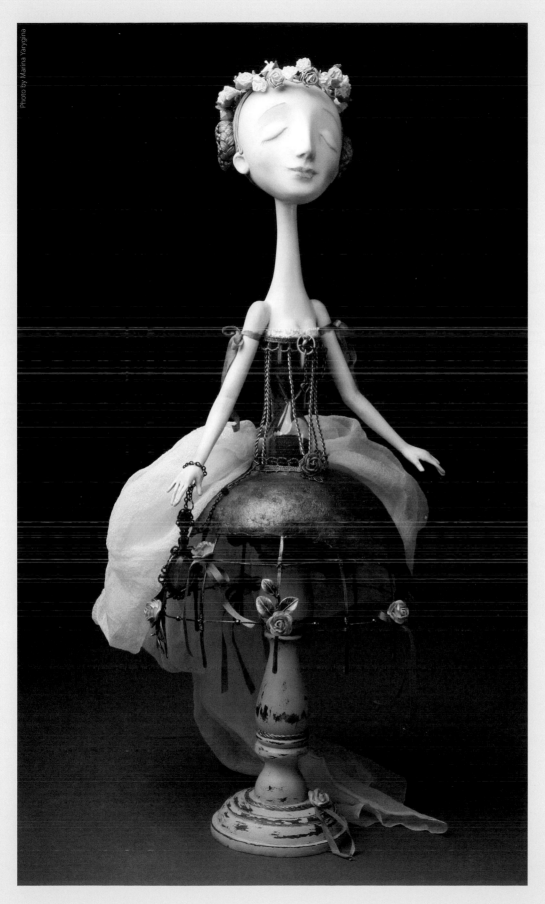

Stop, Time!, *by Yulia Litvinova, 2011*
Made from papier-mâché and mixed media

Alena Eliseeva (Volgograd, Russia)

alena-eliseeva.blogspot.com

Alena Eliseeva is an art doll and toy maker who began making dolls in 2003 and now actively participates in art doll and craft exhibitions. She has experimented with many different materials and creates a variety of fantastic creatures—delicate textile and polymer clay dolls, miniature bears, and dragons.

Photo by Anna Loktionova

Photo by Anna Loktionova

Mityai, *by Alena Eliseeva, 2010*
Made from FIMO

Whisper of the Sea, *by Alena Eliseeva, 2010*
Made from Creative Paperclay

Alisa Bazhenkova
(St. Petersburg, Russia)
www.kukliki.ru

Alisa Bazhenkova graduated from St. Petersburg State University of Technology and Design. She now works as a director of the School of Dolls and teaches a course on air-hardening modeling materials. Since beginning to make art dolls in 2004, she has participated in and won many art doll exhibitions. She has also created Doll Land, her own world filled with fantastic creatures, dolls, interesting characters, and animals.

My Star Far Away, *by Alisa Bazhenkova, 2010*
Made from Creative Paperclay and mixed media

Nanny and Babies, *by Alisa Bazhenkova, 2010*
Made from Creative Paperclay and mixed media

Lubov Nalogina
(Mytishchi, Russia)
takiyaje.livejournal.com

Lubov Nalogina is an
illustrator of children's
books and for the
children's magazine
Kykymber. She collects
vintage dolls and bears,
and she loves to travel
and listen to French
music. She makes tex-
tile dolls and animals
in her own inimitable
style—delightful and
slightly melancholy
creations with realistic
eyes. She pays a great
deal of attention to
details, accessories,
and costumes.

Photos by Lubov Nalogina

Princess, *by Lubov Nalogina, 2011*
Made from textiles

Photos by Lubov Nalogina

Mr. Fox, *by Lubov Nalogina, 2011*
Made from textiles

Ira Krokhmal (Rehovot, Israel)
www.irushka.com

Ira Krokhmal is a professional computer programmer.
For many years she has created textile dolls and toys,
many of which are united in thematic series, such
as Insects, City Angels, and Alice in Wonderland.
She often uses spices for painting and finishing toys,
giving them a wonderful, delicate aroma. She teaches
textile doll courses and participates in many international art doll and craft exhibitions.

Photo by Ira Krokhmal

City Angels, *by Ira Krokhmal, 2011*
Made from textiles

Olivia, *by Ira Krokhmal, 2011*

Made from textiles

Yulia Yurkevich

(St. Petersburg, Russia)

yulia_yu_yu.livejournal.com

Yulia Yurkevich studied the technique of art doll making and then became involved in wool felting and making teddy bears and art toys by hand. She received her training in this art from the leading Russian teddy bear makers. Now Yulia uses the classic techniques of making art bears to create bears from felted wool. She actively participates in exhibitions, teaches a felting course, and writes master classes for various craft magazines.

Kitty, *by Yulia Yurkevich, 2010*
Made from wool

Hedgehog, *by Yulia Yurkevich, 2011*
Made from wool and mohair

Tatjana Grigorjeva
(Moscow, Russia)
ja_ne_user.livejournal.com

Tatjana Grigorjeva graduated from Moscow State Pedagogical University, where she studied biology and chemistry. She started to make art teddy bears in 2003 and came up with her own unique method of making bears from ordinary newspaper. She also makes bears from paper, linen, and other nontraditional materials. Even though she uses unusual materials, she follows the classic techniques for making collectors' teddy bears.

Yasha-Pioneer, *by Tatjana Grigorjeva, 2007*
Made from pages of 1937 newspaper *Pioneer Truth*

The Bear Village: Evynne, *by Tatjana Grigorjeva, 2007*
Made from linen

cinderella princess doll

(project on page 27)

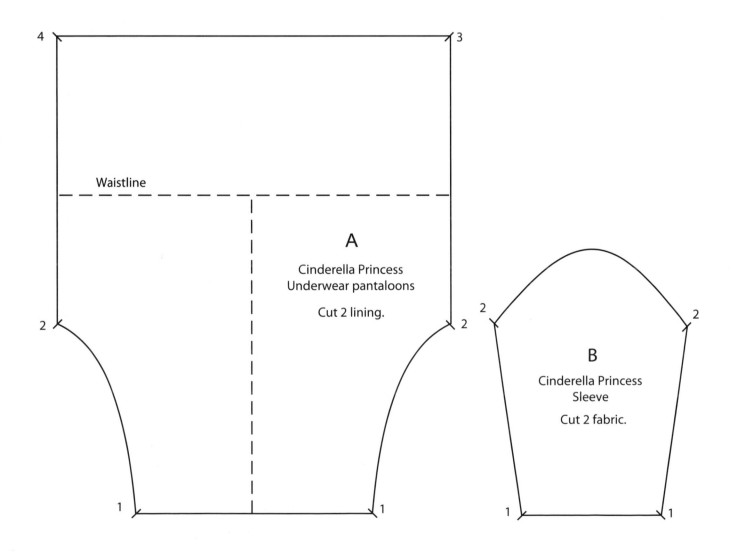

4 ⌐ 3

Waistline

A

Cinderella Princess
Underwear pantaloons

Cut 2 lining.

2 2

1 1

2 2

B

Cinderella Princess
Sleeve

Cut 2 fabric.

1 1

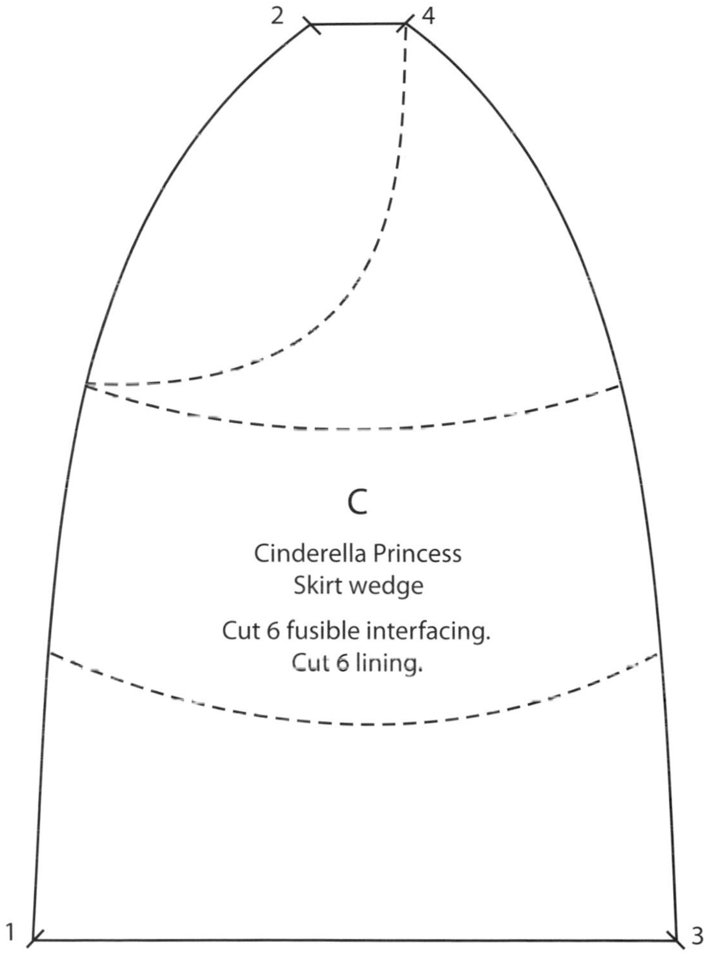

2   **4**

C

Cinderella Princess
Skirt wedge

Cut 6 fusible interfacing.
Cut 6 lining.

1   **3**

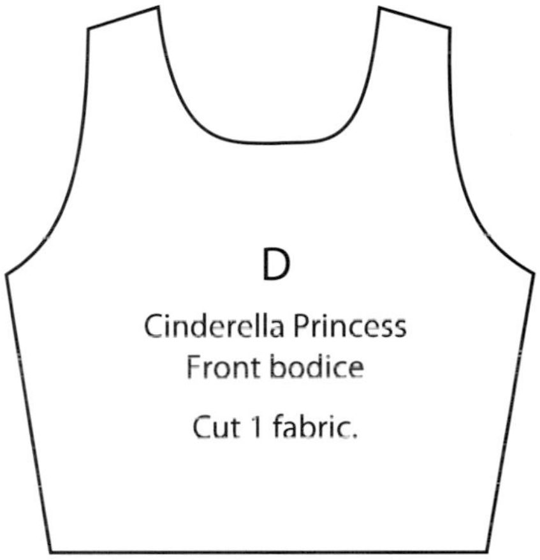

D

Cinderella Princess
Front bodice

Cut 1 fabric.

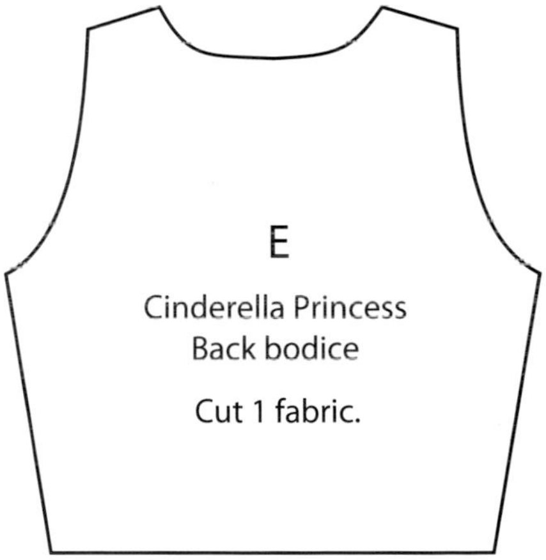

E

Cinderella Princess
Back bodice

Cut 1 fabric.

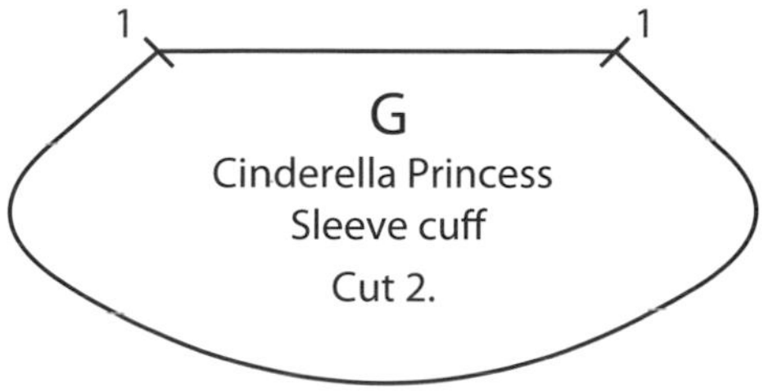

1   **1**

G
Cinderella Princess
Sleeve cuff
Cut 2.

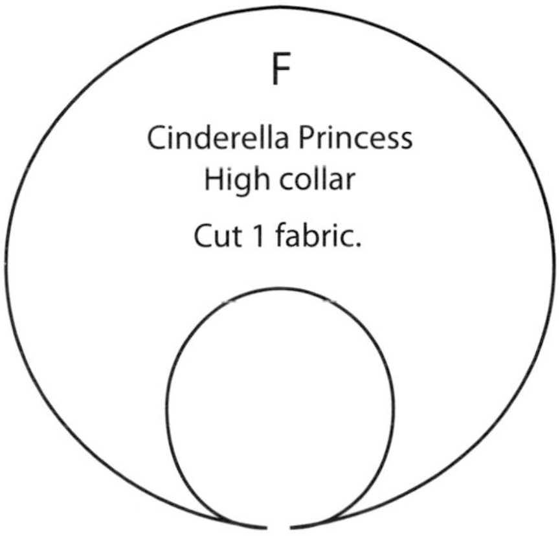

F

Cinderella Princess
High collar

Cut 1 fabric.

rose fairy doll

(project on page 35)

A

Rose Fairy
Leg of pantaloons

Cut 2.

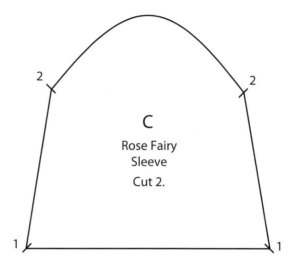

C

Rose Fairy
Sleeve

Cut 2.

B

Rose Fairy
Top of pantaloons and undergarment

Cut 2.

E Rose Fairy
Shoe back   Cut 2.

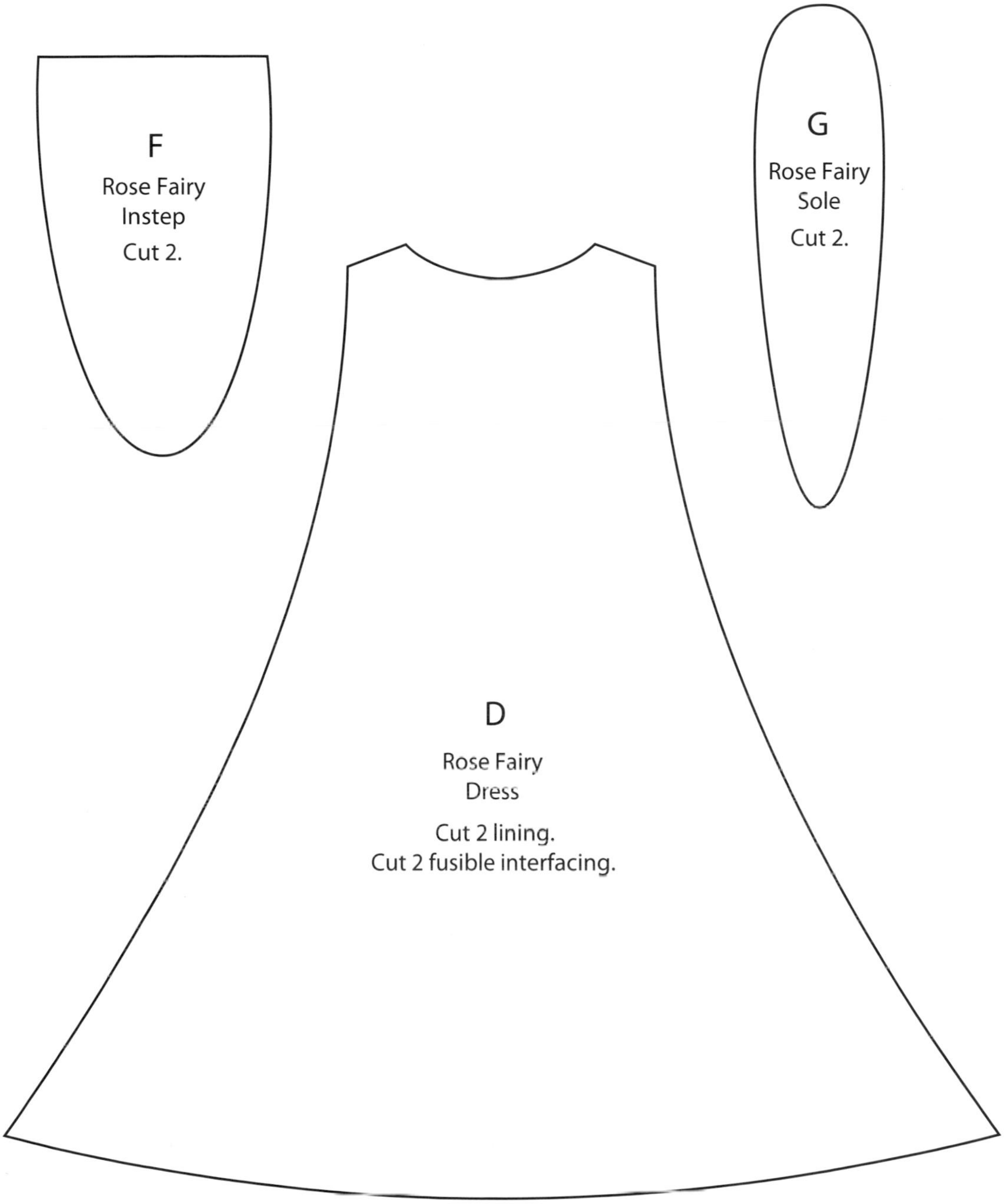

F
Rose Fairy
Instep
Cut 2.

G
Rose Fairy
Sole
Cut 2.

D

Rose Fairy
Dress

Cut 2 lining.
Cut 2 fusible interfacing.

butterfly doll in a frame

(project on page 45)

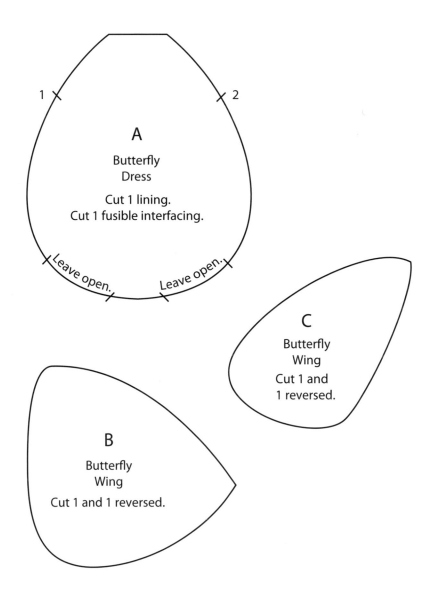

A

Butterfly
Dress

Cut 1 lining.
Cut 1 fusible interfacing.

Leave open.   Leave open.

1   2

C

Butterfly
Wing
Cut 1 and
1 reversed.

B

Butterfly
Wing

Cut 1 and 1 reversed.

fantasy fish

(project on page 52)

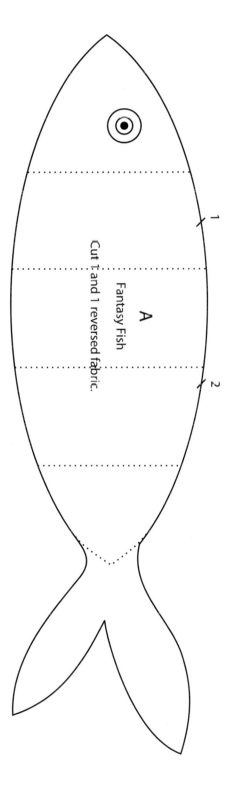

A

Fantasy Fish

Cut 1 and 1 reversed fabric.

brooch doll trio

(project on page 49)

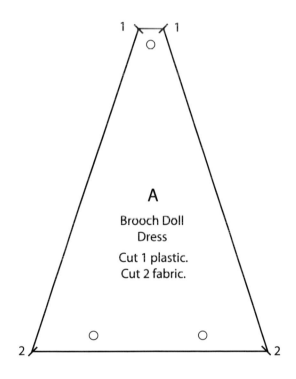

A

Brooch Doll
Dress

Cut 1 plastic.
Cut 2 fabric.

elegant teddy bear

(project on page 55)

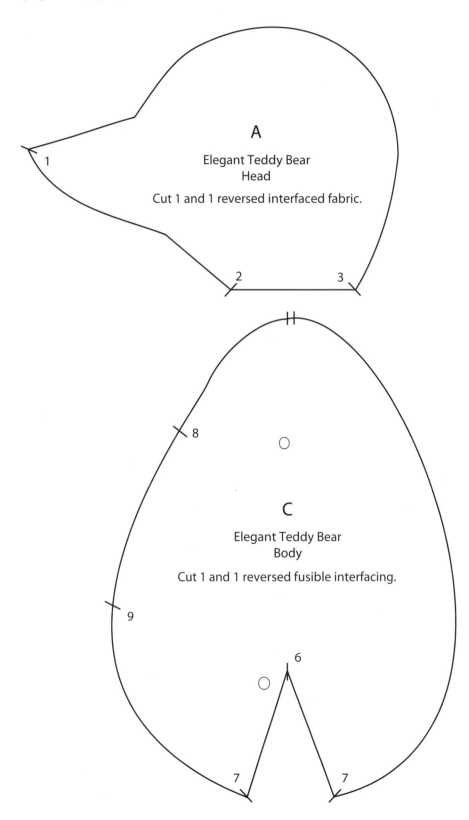

A

Elegant Teddy Bear
Head

Cut 1 and 1 reversed interfaced fabric.

C

Elegant Teddy Bear
Body

Cut 1 and 1 reversed fusible interfacing.

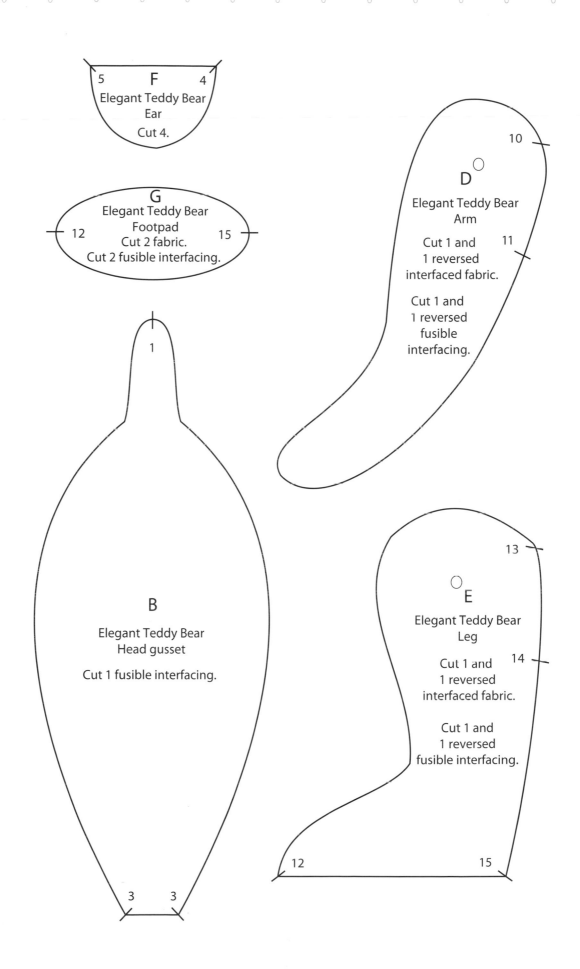

5 F 4
Elegant Teddy Bear
Ear
Cut 4.

G
Elegant Teddy Bear
Footpad
Cut 2 fabric.
Cut 2 fusible interfacing.
12   15

D ○
Elegant Teddy Bear
Arm

Cut 1 and
1 reversed
interfaced fabric.

Cut 1 and
1 reversed
fusible
interfacing.

10

11

1

B

Elegant Teddy Bear
Head gusset

Cut 1 fusible interfacing.

3   3

○
E
Elegant Teddy Bear
Leg

Cut 1 and
1 reversed
interfaced fabric.

Cut 1 and
1 reversed
fusible interfacing.

13

14

12   15

enchanted cottage

(project on page 59)

A

Enchanted Cottage
Front and back wall

Cut 2 fabric.
Cut 2 fusible interfacing.
Cut 2 cardboard.

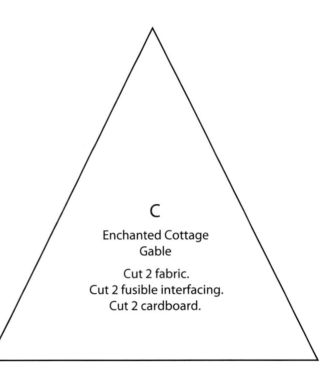

C

Enchanted Cottage
Gable

Cut 2 fabric.
Cut 2 fusible interfacing.
Cut 2 cardboard.

B

Enchanted Cottage
Side wall, roof, foundation

Cut 6 fabric.
Cut 2 fusible interfacing.
Cut 5 cardboard.

resources

Crazy Quilting Books and Online Resources
Aller, Allison Ann. *Allie Aller's Crazy Quilting:
Modern Piecing & Embellishing Techniques for Joyful Stitching.*
C&T Publishing, Inc., 2011.

Baker Montano, Judith. *Judith Baker Montano's Embroidery
& Crazy Quilt Stitch Tool: 180+ Stitches & Combinations
• Tips for Needles, Thread, Ribbon, Fabric • Left- & Right
Handed Illustrations.* C&T Publishing, Inc., 2008.

Causee, Linda. *An Encyclopedia of Crazy Quilt Stitches
and Motifs.* DRG/American School of Needlework, 1997.

*Sharon b's Dictionary of Stitches for Hand Embroidery
and Needlework.* www.inaminuteago.com/stitchindex.html

Art and Craft Stores
Aaron Brothers   www.aaronbrothers.com

Dick Blick Art Materials   www.dickblick.com

Michaels Stores   www.michaels.com

Doll- and Bear-Making Supplies
www.clothdollsupply.com
Patterns, fabrics, trims, tools, and sewing accessories for cloth dolls

www.darwi.com
Darwi Classic air-hardening modeling material

www.decoart.com
All-purpose, premium-quality acrylic paints and varnish

www.faber-castell.com
Watercolor pencils and soft pastels

www.fimo.com
FIMOair air-hardening modeling material

www.glasseyesonline.com
A selection of teddy bear joint sets and eyes

www.hobbylobby.com
*Sculpting tools, various modeling materials, brushes, paints,
and doll accessories*

www.littletrimmings.com
Tiny trimming materials for doll makers

www.minidolls.com
Books, buttons, trims, tools, and sewing accessories

www.miniworlddolls.com
Books, various modeling materials, tools, and doll accessories

www.padico.co.jp
*LaDoll, LaDoll Premix, and LaDoll Premier air hardening
modeling material*

www.paperclay.com
Creative Paperclay

www.plaidonline.com
All-purpose, premium-quality acrylic paints and varnish

About the Author

Photo by Eduarc Druker

Marina Druker was born in the beautiful city of St. Petersburg, Russia, in 1975. From a very early age, she visited the great museums, such as the Hermitage and Peterhof, with her mother. There, she especially loved the exhibitions of decorative and applied arts. Now, many years later, she has come to realize how deeply these experiences affected her own art.

She studied physics at the St. Petersburg State Polytechnical University. In 2003, she moved to Israel, where she met wonderful people and found an occupation that became her favorite—creating dolls. Marina began making dolls using a variety of materials. She settled mainly on sculpting dolls with air-hardening modeling material and creating crazy-quilted costumes. Since 2008, she has also created cloth dolls and crazy-quilted soft sculptures. She has exhibited her dolls internationally.

Marina is moderator of a large Russian-speaking community blog, *All About Dolls*, http://community.livejournal.com/__doll__.

She is also the Israel reporter for the Russian doll magazine *Doll Master*.

Marina lives in Holon, Israel, with her husband and son. You can see more of her works at her website, www.miopupazzo.com.

Great Titles & Products *from* C&T PUBLISHING

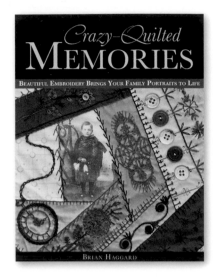

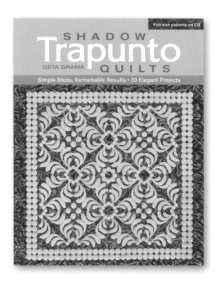

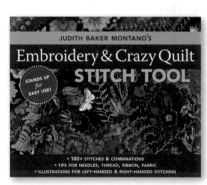

Available at your local retailer or **www.ctpub.com** *or* **800-284-1114**

For a list of other fine books from C&T Publishing, visit our website to view our catalog online.

C&T PUBLISHING, INC.
P.O. Box 1456
Lafayette, CA 94549
800-284-1114

Email: ctinfo@ctpub.com
Website: www.ctpub.com

C&T Publishing's professional photography services are now available to the public. Visit us at www.ctmediaservices.com.

Tips and Techniques can be found at www.ctpub.com > Consumer Resources > Quiltmaking Basics: Tips & Techniques for Quiltmaking & More

For quilting supplies:

COTTON PATCH
1025 Brown Ave.
Lafayette, CA 94549
Store: 925-284-1177
Mail order: 925-283-7883

Email: CottonPa@aol.com
Website: www.quiltusa.com

Note: Fabrics shown may not be currently available, as fabric manufacturers keep most fabrics in print for only a short time.